Malachy Murray's
UNIQUE NEW YORK

From the Stories You Were
Never Told Series

Malachy Murray's
UNIQUE NEW YORK

From the Stories You Were
Never Told Series

Malachy J. Murray (Capt.)

One Broadway Production

For further information, please contact:
Malachy Murray
e-mail at malachymurray@aol.com
http://www.malachymurray.com
http://www.myspace.com/thelaughingwolf

Printed in the United States of America

Malachy Murray's Unique New York:
From the Stories You Were Never Told Series

Malachy J Murray (Capt)

1. Title 2. Author 3. Travel/New York/Guidebook/History

Library of Congress Control Number: 2007927579

ISBN-10: 0-9794691-0-4
ISBN-13: 978-0-9794691-0-7

To the living I am gone,
To the sorrowful, I will never return.
To the angry, I was cheated
But to the happy, I am at peace.
And to the faithful, I have never left.

I cannot speak
But I can listen.
I cannot be seen
But I can be heard.

Remember me in your heart and in your thoughts
For the times we laughed and the times we cried
For the times we loved and for the things we tried.
For the battles I fought and not the way I died.
For if you always think of me, I will have never gone.

"All gave some and some gave all."
09/11/01

Anonymous

POM

My Grandmother who
upon finding out my quest to become a writer;
gave me her first edition signed copy of :

Mark Twain's
A Tramp Abroad

One of many books from her private collection
that now sits on my shelf in my study in an undisclosed location.

POM

Is our Mother,
Grandmother and
Great-Grandmother and
for the grace of our good God
still alive today to see the fruits of her 111 children flourish.

POM

Has many talents.
Learned over the course of ninety some-odd years.
Of them the title of a
Seanache
the Gaelic word for a storyteller.

The art of the telling of a story
has been for years, a long standing trait in our family.
This goes back hundreds of years.
Stories passed down from generation to generation,
told by a skilled tongue and a sharp wit.
Most of them are short, sweet and to-the-point;
yet factual, ironic and always amusing.
Though these stories have survived thousands of years of floods,
wars and famine;
they are now sadly on the brink of extinction.

An oral history of which much of
is forgotten;
maybe forever.
Lost in a new age of a technological
"EVOLUTION"
that has almost eliminated the beauty of the spoken word.

POM

Is one of the last great *Seanaches*.

It is said that
we owe the children of the world,
the voices of our past.
Well…

Welcome to the
"REVOLUTION!"

TABLE OF CONTENTS

INTRODUCTION

In the whole recorded history of mankind, there has
never been another city like New York City. I dare say
that New York City is the greatest city in the world and
of all time. This all of course would depend on how one
would measure greatness. Let's look at some numbers.
The current US census lists New York City as the largest
populated city in America with a booming population
well over 8,100,000. This figure is only a measure of
those who answered the census bureaus request. New
York City is a haven for many people who, for whatever
reason, decide not to stand up and be counted for. This
is a very large and broad counter culture group of people
who range from any number of political dissidents
(Anarchy in the USA!), those with questionable

immigration status (No speaky English!), fleeing fugitives (Don't answer the buzzer till I'm on the fire escape!), illegal tenants (I was born here, REALLY!), wayward businessmen (My office is on 5th Avenue but I have a Delaware address. DON'T ASK!) and last and probably least as well... unemployed actors (Can you get me an agent?)

All this considered; those of us who live here think the population is closer to 10,000,000. People say that because Tokyo has a population of just over 11,000,000 that they are bigger. Well if we were to count the entire New York City Metropolitan area (as they do count the greater Tokyo Metropolitan area) we New Yorkers would easily surpass the 20,000,000 mark. In population, New York City is the largest city in America. Then comes Los Angeles, then Chicago and in fourth place, Houston. New York City is more than twice the size of Los Angeles and bigger than Chicago and Houston combined.

We have three of the eight wonders of the world, right here in New York City. They are; Empire State Building, the Holland Tunnel and the Brooklyn Bridge.

Five boroughs make up New York City. Most people call them counties but we here in the city prefer the word borough. There is Manhattan, the island that most people associate New York with. Then you have Staten Island an island out by the Statue of Liberty. There is

Brooklyn and Queens, they are both on Long Island and then there is the Bronx.

The Bronx is the only borough of the five that is attached to the mainland of America. The other four are islands or part of an island, islands that are here in the largest natural harbor in the world.

With nearly 1000 miles of waterfront property in New York City, it can fit the harbors of London, Amsterdam, Hamburg and Rotterdam all inside of her at the same time. For over three and a half centuries New York City was the busiest commercial shipping port but not since the mid 1960's. In fact, there isn't much commercial shipping in New York anymore. Two things ended commercial shipping here in New York City nearly forty years ago; the forces of Mother Nature and the advances of modern technology had conspired against us. These were, the implementation of containerized shipping, which we will talk about a little later on and the invention of the 747 jumbo jet. Those two things would end commercial shipping in many places but nowhere more so than New York City. Now the only commercial shipping we got left are the ferry boats and the Cruise Liners, when they come into town. Now the Liners don't homeport out of here... yet... But that may still happen, keep your fingers crossed. They visit here and when they arrive, they berth in the last deep water piers of Manhattan. The piers just north of the USS Intrepid museum.

On the pages that follow ahead are many of the stories of what makes New York City so unique. Most of them were obtained from encyclopaedia sources or more of the common accepted pieces of literature on the subject and a good number of them could only be told by someone who "was there" or had lived through the experience. I did my very best to get their facts into ear grabbing stories that I felt got the point across in the best way. I do not have a degree in literature, nor will I make any apologies for that but being a tour guide, I have the unique opportunity to meet thousands of people everyday and listen to their stories. Many of these people I found out to be distant relatives or were in some way akin or connected to some of the characters in this book. It would be, at least in my mind, very selfish to keep these experiences to myself. I am your tour guide. I give the story of our city to everyone who comes on our boats. Now, with this book and the others I hope to write, I can reach the rest of you.

"We either live our dreams or we die in someone else's."

Malachy Murray

PREFACE

What is otherwise known as Superman's Metropolis or Batman's Gotham City is the greatest city in the whole world and of all time; our New York City. It's ours because it belongs to all of us, the whole world; the good the bad and the ugly. Each and every day, hundreds of thousands of people rush into our city to work, visit or play but hundreds come to stay. Though many of us were born here an equal amount were not. We learned in life that more than eighty percent of us will die within fifty miles of where we where born. The exception to this rule would be the intrepid people that come here to take a bite out of *the big apple.* New York is a calling that people have inside of them to follow their dreams. When they get here, it's usually inside of their first five minutes when they have their first "New York" experience.

I was born in Jamaica, Queens and spent a good part of my youth on Long Island, where I got to enjoy the best of both worlds. I remember my first trip into the city and how fascinated I was at the tall buildings in the skyline before my grandfather drove over the bridge. Staring at it from the car window it seemed surreal, like in a fantastical movie. When we got into Manhattan we were in the midst of a traffic jam, right at the foot of the bridge. There was an orchestra of horns blowing and police sirens wailing in the background that didn't seem to be getting any closer. In the front of us was a big, loud and dirty dump truck; a huge version of one of the toys I played with. Then out of nowhere, a bike messenger on a ten-speed bicycle appeared and pounded his fists on the side door of the truck; obviously upset over something. The driver of the truck produced a pipe wrench and threatened the bike messenger with it. Then, in one smooth move, the messenger pulled his chain and lock from under his seat and began swinging it over his head like a cowboy. The two cursed at each other for a moment and then the bike messenger took off without further incident.

Now my mother was almost hysterical with fear but her father, (my grandfather) a self made man as tough as they came, was strangely calm and silent. He told us that this was a typical New Yorker; "he fears no one but respects all." Here was a guy on a bicycle that this big powerful truck could've flattened in one touch of his wheel but the defiant bike messenger was going to get his point across anyway. Whatever his point was, he earned the respect of everyone there watching. This was my first New York experience, and one of the first lessons of life I would learn: *Fear no one but respect all.*

The stories I am telling in this book have more to do with the history of our city. Sure, I promise to have it seasoned with my philosophy, it will read with my bias and my prejudice for it is how I see our city. I am a native New Yorker and outside of my tours in the service, I have lived here all my life. However, most of the history I learned came from my experience as a tour guide on America's favorite boat ride.

How did I get here? Those tour guides are the best in the world. They have to keep their audiences riveted for three hours straight. Who else does this? Stand-up comics don't usually go past fifty minutes, the average "three act" Broadway show is around ninety minutes and most operas are just over two hours... The Circleline is a three hour, one-man show, twice a day and sometimes three; five days a week and sometimes six; the opportunity to work seven days happens to all of us at least once per season. The tours run all year long but depending on your seniority, your stint could be anywhere from three months to the whole year. The seating capacity of the vessels is over 500 which would qualify the show as a "Broadway" production (as opposed to off-Broadway or off-off Broadway) but we

14

operate under the Department of Transportation, not Consumer Affairs and though most of us are actors on the side, the tour doesn't have any affiliation to Actors Equity or any of the theatrical unions. Like the rest of the crew, we are proud members of United Marine Division Local 333 and under the supreme authority of the United States Coast Guard.

Though the days are long and most are hot (no air conditioning in the Harlem River!) The pay is fair and the company treats us well. They know that the people come from all over the world not to see them shuffle paper work, book charter cruises or sell tickets. Nor do they come to see the captains and crews man the vessels, nor the yard birds tinker with the engines in the repair shops. The people come to see us show them our city and we guides are the front lines to the general public. Though every job in the company is important and an intricate part of the well managed machine here; the company understands that it is the passengers who pay our salaries.

Though I have been "guiding" here for five seasons, I am still considered one of the new guides. In fact as far as seniority goes, I am still only number nine in a fleet of eight vessels. I was hired in 1996 when the union hall sent me to Pier 83 on West 42nd Street as a deckhand and worked as a relief when and where ever there was a man down somewhere. My curious nature had me learn all the functions of the operation of the vessel. My relief works included working as the First Mate on deck, the

Oiler in the engine rooms and the Deck-aneer (deckmate/engineer) on the Beast boats when they entered the fleet. Eventually, I sat for my captain's license and am qualified to master vessels up to 100 gross tons in near coastal waters. However my biggest challenge came one day when the ship I was decking on, pulled out of the slip without a tour guide. This was the day that I turned a corner and never looked back.

This particular trip was not our stock in trade, three-hour tour around the island but a private charter booked by a new client. I was on watch, sitting in the wheelhouse when a frantic knock came on the cabin door. I opened the door in haste and was faced with a panicked charter representative asking where the tour guide was. The captain pulled the charter sheet out and after carefully reading it over; he showed the client that there was no guide requested. The charter required nothing special but a three hour tour around the island. On the verge of tears, the client begged the captain to return to the pier to get a tour guide. The captain calmly explained to the client the two major problems with that request.

"I'll do it" I heard myself say, half thinking the captain would say no. To my shock, the captain said "ok" without any hesitation. He did ask me if I was ever a guide before but before I could answer, the client was pushing me out the door to get "mic-ed up". I said "no, but I live here" and the client said that was good enough.

I will never forget the feeling I had when the first mate hooked up the sound system and handed me the microphone for the first time. There wasn't anything ceremonial about it, he handed it to me and said simply, "you're on." I took the microphone and turned to face 544 hot and angry people and I didn't know what to say. Sure, I remembered being scared before. I climbed into "the ring" plenty of times to fight guys twice my size and half my age, or being so cold, that I was afraid to fall asleep some nights for fear of not waking up. I sailed on ships that were knocked around like toys in more than a few Atlantic storms. Many times I was so scared; I thought they would break in half and the angry ocean would swallow us whole. But there was no fear like this fear. This fear was paralyzing, I couldn't move. I tried to hand the microphone back to the first mate and the client but they jumped back as if I just dropped a water balloon.

"Go" the first mate demanded, but I just blanked. I looked to the left of me and then to the right and I couldn't think of anything to say. I forced myself to say hello but even though I had a microphone, I wasn't sure if they heard it; the crowd remained silent. I have never felt so stupid, so undignified or so humiliated in all my life then when I was standing there it what seemed like an eternity. *"How did I get here?"* I heard myself ask myself. I was so nervous that my voice cracked. That, the crowd heard and let out a brisk chuckle. I knew from that, there was only one way out of this – and that was through. I will make them laugh, with me or at me it didn't matter at that point. I wasn't getting anywhere just standing there like a pin cushion.

I pointed to something on the island and told them what it was, and then I told them about a book I had just read on organized crime. They where more interested in the book. I pointed to something else on the island and wondered myself what it was and then I began talking about other books I read that had to do with the city. I slipped in a few jokes that I heard the other guides tell before and they went along with it, for awhile anyway.

I ended the tour with the thrilling story of the brave men who served aboard the USS Intrepid during WWII. I found myself getting a bit emotional near the climax and let them see it. They loved it and gave me a standing ovation. As we pulled in the client asked me for the microphone and told me to stand down at the gang plank. I didn't hear what he told them but almost everyone that came off the vessel that day shook my hand with something green in it. The greenest came from the client himself who encouraged me to study. He told me that he booked charters all the time and that *performance wins over substance* every time.

I was hooked. I went home and immersed myself into study like I never did before. Though I do not have a formal education, I read any and every book I could beg, borrow or steal that had anything to do with New York. My collection grows every day, at the time of this writing I have six and a half milk crates full of books on

New York City alone and I have another two and a half milk crates full of my own personal notes that I wrote on the city. The walls of my tiny one bedroom apartment are lined with shelves, milk crates and bookcases that are over stuffed with books, sometimes two tiers deep. Other than that I have a futon couch, a television and a PC that I call furniture. And that is about it.

Over the next few seasons, I continued to work on the vessels as the "go-to guy" for the company, worked steady on deck but always filled in where needed. It wasn't very often but every once-in-awhile, I was called in as a guide and I jumped at it every chance I got. I don't remember the second, the third or the twentieth time I worked as a guide but I will never forget that first time. I will never forget sitting there on my break with my head in my hands in the company of an angry crowd, thinking of all the people who looked me in the eye that day and asked me simple questions about the city, MY CITY, that I couldn't answer. *"This will never happen again"* was all I thought. I WILL be back.

This book is the first one of what I hope will be many that I can write for you. New York City is the greatest city in the world because of you. You, meaning everyone of you in the world who come here, some every day and some only once to make us the greatest city in the world and the greatest city of all time. Though I was born here, I hold you in high regard that came here from far away places. It is you who

contribute greatly to our city, for what we wouldn't be
without you?

I woke up on the morning of September 11, 2001 the
same way most of the city did and was horrified at what
the world would witness that day. Like most of the
people, a different person woke up inside of me as the
sun finally set on that day. We all witnessed how almost
3,000 people on that day went on with their normal lives
and had them tragically taken from them. I couldn't
help wonder how many of them checked out before
finding their purpose? How many were living their
dream versus someone else's? The reality of that
unholy terror on that day robbed us all of those beautiful
people AND all of their dreams. If that can happen to
them, then it can happen to any one of us.

I am dedicating the rest of my life to living my dream
and following the path of my bliss. I will do this in the
name and in the spirit of those we all lost, that never got
to. Furthermore I will use all of my knowledge, talent
and experience to inspire and motivate as many as I can,
to do the same. I know many may will see me as "full
of myself" but this I see as an acceptable risk. I am not
a hermit nor will I be the crazy old man who dies
selfishly in a pile of books. I will share my knowledge
with all who will listen and praise all of you who are
living YOUR dream… versus someone else's.

"The geology shaped the geography that shaped the industrial economy, that gave birth to the technology that shaped our cities destiny, only possible in a democracy."

David Parker

HISTORY

At the end of the last Ice age, the icecaps melted away and the thawing waterways shaped the geography of New York City. 15,000 years ago, the river we call The Hudson was a fast and furious stream of white water. Our geographical experts tell us that in another 15,000 years into the future, the river will regress back into the form of the white water stream. It is a great time to be alive!

The river we call the Hudson, is known as America's first river. It's the body of water between the Westside of New York's Manhattan and the east coast of the state of New Jersey. One end of the river starts upstate near our Capitol, Albany and the other end flows through the Verrazano-Narrows Strait and into the Atlantic Ocean.

New York's history (of man) starts way back some 11,000 years ago where the first "known" inhabitants were two-legged upright walking humanoids chasing four-legged dinosaurs slipping and sliding across the icecaps. They were the hunters and gatherers of the day and no doubt there was trading and banking even back then. Popular belief has it that this race of people migrated over the then frozen Bering Strait of Alaska. They then headed east and stopped when they hit the ocean. This tells us that the Native Americans knew that the earth was round first, they walked across it!

The Native Americans here had an oral history that was passed on generation after generation and it spoke of how one day they would meet up with the white men once again. That was a fact that probably turned into a myth after several generations and then when the Vikings landed, like most things in this world that go full circle, it turned back into hard fact once again.

THE VIKINGS

The Vikings were mostly people from the Scandinavian countries who set out to explore the world. The very word "Viking" would strike a chord of fear through the hearts of those living in any of the coastal cities world wide. Most Vikings were merciless, marauding raiders that would take anything they wanted from the coastal cities they landed in. They were especially interested records that the towns kept. When they got what they wanted, they left usually with a few more passengers than they arrived with as Vikings frequently pursued the slave trade.

The Vikings were also excellent navigators. When they couldn't sail along the shores anymore, they picked up their ships and carried them across the land until they found water again! They were never short of volunteers to help them do this, most cities were only too happy to do whatever they could to get these Vikings out of their cities. They kept great records of their journeys and shared charts with other Vikings. Then by the end of the eighth century, the Vikings raided Ireland. This would change things in exploration for all mankind.

The Vikings discovered in their raid, the records of an Irish saint who himself was an explorer. They read about St. Brendan and his monks' journeys across the Atlantic Ocean and how they found land on the other side of her back in the 6th Century. Many people today believe that St. Brendan did discover America but historians find this difficult to prove. St. Brendan's boat was barely larger than a canoe and would never have made the trans-Atlantic journey with his crew and provisions. The land St. Brendan wrote about closely fits the description of the Islands in the Atlantic that surround Ireland and they think he may have gotten as far as Iceland but further journey than that would have been nearly impossible. This didn't matter to the Vikings, for they believed that "*they who dare, conquer*", and dare and conquer they did. It wasn't long after that, that the Vikings pointed their long boats west into the Atlantic Ocean and reaped the wild wind!

The Viking stories are best told in the *Saga of Eric The Red.* This chronicles the voyages of the Vikings that came to America. In it, it talks of a Viking named Thorfinn Karlsefini who was the first European to sail down the river we know today as the Henry Hudson River. Although Thorfinn was as "Viking" as one could get, he had an ulterior motive. He might have been the first one on record to want to colonize this new continent. He Sailed to Greenland and married, Gudrid, the widow of Thorstein; one of Eric the Red's sons! Then he took 160 men and some women including Eric The Red's daughter, Freydisi and sailed for the new land.

It is on record that in the year 1010 Thorfinn and Gudrid's son, Snorri was the first Anglo-European born on this continent. Tragically their son was killed by some of the natives in a raid on their new colony. There was also a lot of "in-fighting" amongst the colonists; most of the spats had to do with the women (apparently there weren't enough of them). After the third winter the colony had imploded and was abandoned and the Karlsefini's and a few of the surviving colonists made it back over to Greenland.

CHRISTOPHER COLUMBUS

Christopher Columbus gets credit for discovering
America? Let's take a closer look at history, as we
know it. After the fall of Constantinople and the
miserable loss of the hundred years wars, the European
Kings had to send explorers *by sea* to Asia to continue
the spice trades. Going over land was now much too
difficult and very risky. Frequent raids on their caravans
by the Ottoman Empire's soldiers didn't make the land
route cost effective. The next best thing was to sail.
The common route was a long and arduous voyage all
the way around Africa through the Cape of Good Hope
and then across the Indian Ocean. Chinese traders tried
to sail from Asia but only got as far as East Africa. Not

cost effective enough for them to trade. The Europeans would have to come to them.

It was discovered by the Portuguese that the further west they sailed into the Atlantic Ocean the faster it was to make it around Africa. Strong currents off of the West African coast were easier to negotiate if they just sailed *around* them. Some Portuguese sailors sailed a bit too far west and landed on Brazil in South America. They discovered this continent by accident. More embarrassed than excited about this discovery, they took what they needed and headed back out for Africa. Then along came Christopher Columbus.

Columbus was born in 1451 in Genoa, Italy in a time where tensions were mounting between the Freemason Kings of Europe and the Holy See (Pope) of Rome. He was the oldest of five children. Columbus ended his formal education at the age of fourteen and spent much of his childhood in different business endeavors with his two younger brothers. The boys loved going to sea and when they weren't sailing they were drawing navigational charts and did quite a bit of business selling them.

Christopher Columbus took one or more voyages around the Cape of Good Hope and experienced how long and difficult it was. *There has got to be a shorter way*, he would think. This idea would burn in his head for years to come. He married the daughter of one of the Governors of Portugal, a man who was himself, a very high degree Freemason and an excellent storyteller. He would fill the young Columbus's head with stories of the Viking voyages and a land across the Atlantic Ocean. A land that Columbus, no doubt, would believe to be China. Upon the death of his young bride, Columbus would sail off to Ireland, Wales and Iceland and then wherever his voracious appetite for Viking intelligence led him. Like a man possessed, Columbus was determined to find a shorter route to the Far East via the Atlantic Ocean.

Most of the people back in the 1400s referenced a map drawn by Ptolmy, a second century Egyptian astronomer / mathematician / philosopher as to what the world was; flat and surrounded by water but not much of it. This contradicted what Columbus learned in his study of the Vikings. Columbus returned to Portugal and pitched his trans-Atlantic voyage to find China's backdoor, to King John II. Although impressed with Columbus's esoteric knowledge, King John II was only interested in finding a faster way around Africa. He dismissed Columbus's idea, not because he thought the Earth was flat but because the King knew the voyage was a lot more (25%) than Columbus said it was and wasn't confident enough that his ships could make a journey that long. Columbus turned his nose up at the King, rolled up his charts and goose-stepped over to the Portuguese rival, the Spanish.

Spain had kept under the influence of the Holy See. Queen Isabella's close council of advisors was made up of Franciscan friars and a consortium of other holy

people. Columbus being Catholic and Italian found
better luck there. When the Friars asked Columbus what
he would do with his proceeds from the voyage,
Columbus vowed to liberate Jerusalem from Muslim
rule, rebuild the Jew's holy temple and bring on a new
age of the holy spirit! This won him huge favor from
the council. Though the Spanish too had rejected
Columbus's idea at first, so impressed was Queen
Isabella, that she put Columbus on her payroll. Within a
few short years, Columbus's persistence would pay off.
He had a fleet of 3 ships and a crew ready to set sail
west on the Atlantic Ocean. A voyage that would
endure many hardships, including several mutiny
attempts. Columbus, in all his single-mindedness,
finally reached the Americas. On that historical day in
October of 1492, when Columbus landed in San
Salvador, the world gives credit to him for discovering
the new world but Columbus actually did more than that.
His tunnel-vision view of a shorter route to Asia got the
two major powers of Europe together to take interest in
the new world. He got them interested in the cash crops
like tobacco, rubber, sugar and many others, opening
doors to trade with both the natives and each other.

Christopher Columbus may not have been the first
European on the North American continent but by
bringing two worlds together; the powers of Europe with
the goods of the Americas, a new world had begun!

GIOVANNI Da VERRAZANO

Though Christopher Columbus never landed in New York or anywhere near it; it would be nearly a century before this city was discovered. In the year 1524 a Florentine named Giovanni Da Verranzano, sailing under the French flag discovered this harbor. Unfortunately he never set foot on the ground here but he named the river that we call the Hudson River after his idol, Christopher Columbus.

Giovanni and his brother Girolamo, a map maker, were on board one of four ships that left France en route to the Americas for an expedition in the new world. Two of the ships were lost at sea and another turned back after raiding a Spanish galleon, so Giovanni's ship the *Dauphine* was the only one to make it to the new world. When they came to the opening of the Hudson River, they anchored the ship outside of the strait now named

The Giovanni Da Verrazano-Narrows Strait and lowered himself into a boat with a few oarsmen and paddled into the harbor. He wrote about how he saw natives with different color feathers in their hair and dressed in colorful beads and how they seemed cheerful to meet them, paddling out around the harbor in canoes. Just then a strong gust of wind began to kick up and Giovanni decided to head back to his ship. He had already lost the other three ships and didn't want to risk the King's flagship. For fear of the Spanish, Giovanni had a habit of anchoring much further out to sea than most ships usually did. This would come back to haunt him later in his life.

Giovanni returned to France reporting to the King his discoveries and would make several more voyages across the Atlantic. Like his idol Columbus, Giovanni encountered many hardships on these voyages. Once when his crew mutinied and ordered him to sail back to France, he used their ignorance in navigation against them by sailing to Brazil. There, Giovanni found rare trees of the rainforest that he cut down and took back to the King. However when the King sent him back in 1528 for some more wood, Giovanni never made it back. He anchored out too far (as he usually did) somewhere off the coast of what is believed to be the Antilles today. The natives that he thought were friendly turned out to be cannibals. They killed him and his landing party before they reached the shore and ate him in front of his brother who was back on the ship, too far out of firing range to help them.

MANHATTAN

Manhattan is the name of New York County. It is one of the five boroughs that most people refer to when they say New York City. It is the only borough of the five that keeps its original Native American name. *Manhattan* loosely translates to *"Island of hills and trees."* Other tribes have translated it to *"Island of the plenty"* or even *"Island of decadence."* Native Americans who lived here for thousands of years before the Europeans, used to come from hundreds of miles around, several times a year to trade their goods with other tribes. They used this island as their primary hunting grounds, held elaborate feasts and performed sacred rituals with each other. For as long as humans set foot on this island it was always a melting pot, where hundreds of cultures collided, yet co-existed.

Manhattan itself is just about twenty-two square miles in area. This makes Manhattan the smallest county in all of America. Yet the smallest county in all of America hosts over 3,000,000 people a day. It is estimated that 1.5 million people live here and an equal amount who come in everyday to work or visit. Also, the smallest county in all of America hosts the most skyscrapers. Every major company, corporation, bank and business owns a skyscraper and most of them are here in Manhattan. Most of them are right here in our midtown. In fact, midtown Manhattan is the largest downtown in the world and our downtown Manhattan is the third largest downtown in the world. The second largest one is in Chicago, where ironically skyscrapers started, but we have more of them here. So this island, just over twenty-two square miles in are hosts the first and the third largest downtowns in the world along with 3,000,000 people from all over the world. This all comes courtesy of a gift we got from Mother Nature.

Mother Nature blesses us all with special gifts. Each and every one of us are all born with some sort of greatness. The unique ability to do something great is in all human beings. This is a gift we are given, a talent called by many "genius". This genius is different in everyone; this is what makes us unique unto each other and it can be suggested that it is why we need each other.

"Hide not your talents, they for use were made. What's a sun-dial in the shade?"

UNIQUE NEW YORK

Benjamin Franklin

However, it is said that eighty-five percent of us will live out our entire lives without ever even finding out what our genius is. That is eighty-five percent of us go to our graves at the end of our lives with our best "song" still in us. This leaves just fifteen percent of the people in the world to rule the rest. That is the basis of today's stories. It is about those fifteen percent of the people who found out what their genius was and they came here to New York City and put their names on something here. It's something that made us the greatest city in the world and the greatest city of all time and something that we are going to remember these people for; for a long time to come. Hopefully after this book, you folks will be inspired to go out in our city here and visit these sites. Perhaps find out what your genius is and get a chance to leave something here behind with your name on it. Something we will all remember you for, for a long time to come, if you haven't done this already.

Mother Nature blessed Manhattan with a number of special gifts. One of them is her bedrock foundation. Bedrock is some of the hardest natural substance on this planet. This bedrock is what gives us the ability to build skyscrapers. That is why the skyscrapers are in Manhattan and not so much the other four boroughs or in much of the mainland of America. The bedrock in Manhattan is the right type for skyscrapers and in the right location, just below the surface. Just about everywhere else, you need to dig down too deep to get to the bedrock. Now a skyscraper is any building over twenty-two stories. Once you go up that high, the rule is that you need to dig down half as high as you go up, otherwise you'll get something like the leaning tower of Pisa all over again. Going down eleven stories into the ground just to go up twenty-two stories in the sky isn't cost effective. But when bedrock is your foundation, you need only dig down fifty-five feet. That is how massive and dense that bedrock is. Fifty-five feet down and you could build up just about as high as you like. You probably wouldn't do that for a number of reasons, skyscrapers kind of have a glass ceiling at 100 stories. Ironically the very thing that makes skyscrapers possible, elevators is the same thing that limits their height. Anything built over 100 stories tall and the elevator use becomes too time consuming. This is why we started building skyscrapers in sets of two, hence the Twin Towers.

THE HUDSON RIVER

The river we call the Hudson, is known as America's
first river. It's the body of water between the Westside
of Manhattan Island and the east coast of the State of
New Jersey (and technically the State New York as
well). One end of the river starts upstate past our
capitol, Albany to a lake in the Adirondack Mountains
called *Tear in the Clouds* and the other end flows
through the Verrazano-Narrows Strait and out into the
Atlantic Ocean. The Native American's, who lived here
for thousands of years before the Europeans came,
named this river the Muhheakunnuk *(Muh-he-kun-ne-
tuk)* River, which loosely translates to *"river with lots of
trouble"* or *"river that flows both ways."* Both ways,
there is lots of trouble in this river; current wise and
otherwise. The ice flows from the peaks of the

Adirondack Mountains and the freshwater lakes upstate melt and rush down mixing here with the salt water tides from the Atlantic Ocean, colliding yet co-existing. So the New York City section of the Hudson River is both fresh and salt water. This is something we call brackish. It makes for the most interesting collection of wildlife too. We have both fresh and salt water swimmers here, colliding, yet co-existing. This arrangement of harmony or energy is something the Chinese call, *"Feng Shui."* It's a harmony (or an energy) of forces that start here in our river and spills over onto the island of Manhattan. An island that hosts a forest of skyscrapers of all different shapes, sizes and colors; representing the people of all the different races, creeds, colors and religions of the world, that come from all over to make there mark here with us, in New York City.

As the cliché goes; New York City is one huge melting pot, a human laboratory of social and economical sciences. Hence the question: *"Can all of the different peoples of the world come together in one city and prosper?"*

Well, we are going to find out.

HENRY HUDSON

Hendrick (Henry) Hudson, an Englishman sailing for the Dutch on an eighty ton ship called *De Haelve Maen* (The Half Moon) with a mixed crew of Dutch and English sailors were the first Europeans to set foot in New York City.

Hendrick Hudson was one of eight boys born into a considerably wealthy family in England. His father and grandfather owned the Muscovy Shipping company where all eight boys were employed in various departments. Young Henry, as you might imagine, loved to sail and became one of the company's finest navigators. He and his wife Kathrine had three sons; Richard, Oliver and John. It would be John to accompany his father on his voyages to the new world, serving as the ships cabin boy.

Like Christopher Columbus, Henry Hudson had a vision of a shorter route to Asia. Where Columbus thought he could find it by sailing west, Hudson thought he could find it by sailing north. Somewhere through the icecaps of the North Pole was the fabled Northwest Passage. Captain John Smith, who set up the English colony in Jamestown, Virginia, corresponded with Hudson. In one of his letters, he told Hudson about a river on the east coast of the new world below 40` latitude. The Reverend Samuel Purchas, Hudson's spiritual advisor, told Hudson that in the land of the midnight sun where the sun shines for five months, the icecaps thaw clearing a "river" to the Far East. This, coming from Purchas, a man who never traveled much more than fifty miles from his birthplace and used twisted interpretations of biblical scripture to support his arguments, somehow convinced Hudson and the Muscovy Shipping Company to launch an expedition to find the fabled *"Northwest Passage"*; the "river" to the Far East.

Time is money and saving time means saving money and money is the name of the game. ALWAYS! Even Henry Hudson and his wife Kathrine opened up a boarding house to earn some extra cash. England, like most of the European countries, were strapped for cash. Voyages around the Cape of Good Hope were long, expensive, dangerous and very risky. They tried building faster ships but faster usually meant lighter or weaker. Lighter ships couldn't hold as much bounty, couldn't fight off pirates as well and were often lost in storms.

With the dawn of the Age of Discover came piracy. Countries found it easier to just raid each other's ships of the booty. It was a lot easier than going all the way around the cape and back. Raids were always a concern for any crew anywhere on the high seas. Sure there were treaties between countries but that hardly mattered. Privateers, did "legal" raids, illegal raids were done by pirates. If a "friendly" ship was in view, the Captain could just raise the black flag, dress his crew like marauders and seize the ship. That was called piracy and everybody justified it because every country lost ships. Sometimes whole ships and crews were captured. The longer a ship stayed out at sea the greater chance it had of disappearing. So everybody was in a race – to find a quicker route.

Voyages around the cape were expensive but in the big picture, profitable. Voyages to nowhere or uncertainty, like what Columbus and Hudson proposed, where few and far between. Charters like that were only awarded to those who could convince the Crown it would one way or another, pay-off. Hudson's reputation as a navigator and top mariner proceeded him significantly; enough to get the green light on the voyage to find the Northwest Passage. As it turned out, voyages to uncertainty weren't awarded the best ships. The Crown wasn't going to risk neither her newest ship nor her finest crew. Hudson would command the Hopewell with a crew of twelve; one of them would be his fifteen year-old son, John.

Hudson returned from that voyage unsuccessful but he was able to chart his journey quite accurately and pin point specific whaling sights. Whaling was a less than but quite profitable industry. For all Hudson's maritime genius, he lacked basic leadership skills. Hudson's crew, most of them surly ex-cons from debtor's prisons, didn't find the Arctic cold interesting for very long. They threatened him with mutiny and furthermore, forced Hudson to draft and sign a letter saying there was no mutiny attempt and that Hudson turned back under his own volition!

Satisfied with Hudson's new charts and whaling sights, three months later the Muscovy Trading Company sent Hudson out again to find that Northwest Passage. Among this crew would be Hudson's son John and new First Mate, Robert Juet, a man described by Hudson as *"a man with mean tempers"*. For all that Juet was good at seamanship, he lacked in many of the common or social graces. Again problems with the crew and a mutiny would threaten and again, unsuccessful in finding the Northwest Passage, Hudson returned to England.

Nobody in England was interested in sending out Hudson again after his two failures, they lost interest. Though Hudson slipped in and out of a depression, he never lost hope; the Reverend Purchas wouldn't let him. In fact it was Purchas who got Hudson to meet with the Dutch Ambassador. When Hudson felt his own countrymen failed him, he simply did what Columbus did and went over to his country's [England's] rival, in this case the Dutch.

The Dutch, like everyone else in Europe, were interested in finding a quicker way to the Far East and although they found Hudson's idea considerably risky, they hired him for fear that he might go over to their other rivals, the French and bid.

The Dutch East India Shipping Company gave Hudson command of *De Haelve Maen* (The Half Moon) another eighty-ton square-rigged vessel that rode high in the water and blew around like a kite at the mercy of the wind. He had a mixed crew of nineteen Dutch and English men including his son John and again, for reasons never made clear, the quarrelsome Juet as Master's Mate. Juet was at constant odds with the mixed crew, including Hudson, himself. With Juet as the head instigator, the Dutch and English sailors were constantly fighting with each other. Hudson couldn't be bothered; he was focused on finding the fabled "Northwest Passage" and just let the crew be. He rarely disciplined them and even showed blatant signs of favoritism. When the crew no longer tolerated the icy arctic weather, it was Juet who led the mutiny. This time Hudson did what Giovanni Da Verrazano did, tricked his crew and headed for the new world.

The Muhheakunnuk River is what the Algonquin natives called, what we today call, the Hudson River. It loosely translates to "river that flows both ways". Henry Hudson sailed the Half Moon through the Giovanni Da Verrazano Strait and into the New York City Harbor. He saw the river disappear over the arc of the curve of the Earth and thought he found that fabled Northwest Passage. Elated, he wrote in his logbook "This will be the date we alter history." This would be September 11, 1609. Remember this date.

Natives dressed in mantles of colorful feathers, furs and beads boarded the ship and offered Hudson fresh tobacco and corn. Hudson noticed how naturally fortified the harbor was and sailed further up north. He stopped near the Tappan Zee and went ashore where he noticed how fertile the grounds were. He thought that they could grow anything they wanted in this soil. This, along with how generous the natives were in trading their fur pelts away for the steel blades of the crew's knives were logged in Hudson's book. The querulous Juet didn't trust the natives and was the constant instigator in the many skirmishes Hudson and his crew would encounter along the trek up the river. At one point they kidnapped two natives and planned to bring them back as souvenirs. The natives would attack a number of times and somewhere in these scuffles, one native escaped and one was killed. They sailed all the way up to Albany, where Hudson gave up hope. He saw that the river grew too narrow and too shallow so he turned back. He wrote in his journal that this body of water was *"only a river"*.

Up to 100 natives paddled out to the Half Moon and attacked it so Hudson ordered the crew to fend them off with firepower. The Half Moon survived the ambush but at the cost of, at least one crewman and had two others seriously wounded. A number of natives were killed in the attack and it would be long remembered by the natives when the Dutch came to colonize fifteen years later.

Hudson sailed back to Europe and for reasons never fully explained; he stopped off in London instead of sailing straight to Amsterdam. While there, Hudson and his English crewmembers were placed under arrest for sailing under the commission of a foreign vessel. The Dutch crew, were allowed to sail onward to the Netherlands. Here Henry Hudson was placed under house arrest. There was wide speculation that Hudson was employed by England as a spy. England was desperate to find out the Dutch sailing routes. Then why did Hudson venture to the new world rather than head home, after the attempted mutiny? Perhaps he was a spy for the Dutch on the English colony in Virginia? Perhaps could have been both, a double agent? Would a man so possessed in finding the Northwest Passage sell-out his own country, if that is what it took to get back at sea?

Our historians will debate this in the years to come. However, while under house arrest, Hudson managed to send the Dutch Ambassador his discoveries. Though he came up short in finding the Northwest Passage, he convinced the Dutch Government to set up a colony in the area now known as "New York".

A gentleman by the name or Sir Thomas Smythe, Treasurer of the Virginia Company and of the English East India Shipping Company needed to recoup his losses after a disastrous turn-out on his last outing. Smythe gave Hudson command of the *Discovery* and a crew of twenty-two English sailors. Amongst the crew were Henry's son John and for a third time (sigh) the ever-so truculent, Juet.

The crew was as quarrelsome as usual and though Hudson gained oodles of experience in his maritime abilities, he seemed to lose ground in leadership. He never understood how to properly discipline a crew. When the cold got to be unbearable the crew, rife for a mutiny, this time carried it out. The older and wiser Juet successfully manipulated the most of the crew to side with him and take over the ship. They lowered Henry Hudson into a small boat with his son John and several others and cast them adrift into the frozen Arctic Ocean, never to be seen again. On the way back, Inuits killed most of his crew and Juet starved to death. Of the twenty-two men who sailed off at the beginning of that ill-fated voyage, only three returned to England. None of the survivors were ever charged with the mutiny.

For years Katherine, Hudson's wife, fought with the different trading companies for justice and compensation for her loss and finally sued them for a nice chunk of change. She passed away in 1624 the same year the Dutch decided to colonize the New York area of the new world. It would be called "New Amsterdam". Ironically she was buried on September 11th, the same date where fifteen years before, Henry Hudson thought he had altered history. Remember I told you to remember that date.

The Henry Hudson Bridge hooks up to the Henry Hudson Parkway, crosses over the Harlem Shipping Canal in a tiny pocket called the Henry Hudson Cove and parallels the Henry Hudson River. There's also a statue of Henry Hudson in Henry Hudson Park in that area. We named quite a few things in New York City after Captain Henry Hudson; he gets credit for being the first European to bring Europe to this part of the world. Sadly for Henry Hudson, he never lived to see his fame, like Edgar Allen Poe, he was dead long before he became famous.

However Henry Hudson had two other sons, one Oliver and one Richard and their descendants are living amongst us today somewhere in this city. Hudson's son Richard, ironically, made a fortune sailing around Africa. He was so successful in trading that Richard Hudson was one of the first Europeans given a permit to live in Imperial Japan. He lived out a long life of

46

privilege, wealth and prestige. One might guess that he opted for the sure thing. Remember the old Aesop's fable of the Tortoise and the Hare? *"Slow and steady wins."*

NEW AMSTERDAM

As most of you know, New York wasn't always called New York. The first Europeans to set up a colony here were the Dutch. They called their colony New Amsterdam and a man named Peter Minuet was their first Governor. He set up an office on One Broadway, which is the oldest official address in America today. It's also the name of my production company and website: onebroadwayproductions.com.

Governor Minuet as well as all of the Dutch Governors who'd follow after him were under a lot of pressure to make lots and lots of money. For this is something that the Dutch are still known for today for they are one of the wealthiest countries in Europe today.

Discovering the new world was one thing but colonizing it would be yet another. The English colonies set up in Virginia as well as the Connecticut and Massachusetts area we call today, New England. The Dutch claim in the new world was what New York is today, counting Long Island and the east coast all the way down to the Chesapeake Bay area. They called this area New Netherlands and from 1624- 1664 ruled it with crown appointed governors. That's right, none of these tyrannical iron fisted bosses where elected by the colonists, they where chosen by the moneyed folks back in the old country, sowing the seeds of resentment right from the start.

Peter Minuet would be the first official Governor. Born in Germany in 1580, his family fled Spanish persecution and fled to the Netherlands. He became what was called a "Walloon" (Belgian, French speaking Protestant). He was a member of the Dutch West India Company who raided Spanish ships from the West African coast to the New World. While the Netherlands were fighting for their independence from Spain, they were already setting up their claims in the new world. As Hudson promised, fur was a huge commodity in the trade business with the natives. The Dutch West India was making huge profits. How huge? One writer made the comparison to Bill Gates' Microsoft company. Microsoft was showing investors a 30% - 35% profit every year. That made Bill Gates the richest man in the world with a personal worth at about 60 Billion dollars and provided a boon to our economy. The Dutch West India Company was showing their investors 200% – 300% yearly profits!

There it was, the birth of Capitalism in our new nation, over two-hundred years before it was even called (America's) New York. It was without a doubt that the new world is where the money was to be made but with a Dutch Economy so flush, who in the Netherlands wanted to leave the good life, a beautiful home to travel across a violent and unforgiving ocean only to live on raw land amongst savages? This dilemma caused the Dutch West India Company to offer generous land tracts to those who would make the trip over to the new world AND STAY! The first to take advantage of this were the Walloons. Then others fleeing from religious persecution would follow.

Where the Dutch and their economic boon had to pay people to come over to the new world, the English, who were not so flush had a whole other idea on how to colonize the new world. They would simply empty their debtors' prisons and workhouses. Those people were given the opportunity to work off of their debt by cultivating the English Colonies abroad. So either way you look at it, people from Europe began coming to the new world for any number of different reasons.

On May 4, 1626 Peter Minuet arrived in New York and began setting up a colony. The first thing he did was take advantage of the warring native tribes. The Mohawks and the Mohican's were fighting over trading rights with the Dutch settlers. The greed spread like wild fire between the many different tribes and fierce bloody battles broke out between them all over the fur trade. Everything from beavers to bears, seals and otters, raccoons, foxes and on and on were traded for axes, knives, nails or just about anything metal.

Peter Minuet was ordered by the shipping companies to buy Manna-Hatta (Manhattan Island) from the natives so he could put all the colonists on it and they would be out of the way of the warring tribes. The Canarse Indians under Chief Gowanus, sold this land they rarely used anyway to Minuet for 60 Dutch guilders (about $24.oo in today's money) and called the island, New Amsterdam. The Native Americans looked at the island of Manhattan much differently than the Dutch settlers did. To the natives, Manhattan was an island that they didn't settle on but had to commute to. That meant navigating the troubled currents of her rivers in handmade canoes. Manhattan, to the natives, had become an island whose woods were over hunted and whose bedrock foundation made any decent farming impossible. Now the Dutch didn't need that island for either of those purposes. Lucky for the Dutch, the Native Americans were not at all seafaring people and therefore couldn't see the potential of Manhattan's naturally fortified harbor. The Dutch lead the world, still today in the ability to build boats. *Feadship Yachts*, a Dutch company of boat builders stand unrivaled in their ability to build what are called the "Rolls Royce"

of yachts. They boast that every *Feadship Yacht* ever
built is still afloat.

However the natives didn't share the same concept of
real estate that the Dutch did and therefore didn't quite
understand the fact that when they sold Manhattan, they
had to leave the island. Not to say anything about the
other tribes who frequently used the island and didn't
receive any money for it. So the Dutch built a colony at
the southern tip of the island and erected a wall around it
separating it from the rest of the island. Those chosen to
build that wall would be the first African slaves in the
colony. That wall was where Wall Street is today.

Minuet's idea might have worked out well on paper but
reality was another story. In a lesson that history will
repeat over and over again; that walls aren't very
effective alone. Minuet's wall was made out of wood,
wood that the colonists would rather use reinforcing
their own homes. So the slaves would toil at the wall all
day only to have colonists tearing it down at night,
stealing the coveted wood for themselves. The wall was
ineffective in saving the colonists from the natives from
the north and later it would be equally ineffective
against the conquering British from the south. But
today, we call it Wall Street anyway.

The first Dutch Governor was Peter Minuet and the last
one was Peter Stuyvesant. There were several less
remembered ones who served in between the famous

Peters but none as remembered as "Old Silver Nails",
Stuyvesant.

A former soldier, Stuyvesant was given that moniker for
the silver bands around his peg leg. He had lost his real
leg in a battle against the Portuguese down in the West
Indies three years prior to taking over governorship of
New Amsterdam. He took the Dutch colony over when
he was fifty-five years old and for the next seventeen
years he ruled it with an iron fist. Though the colony
was still a rowdy seaport before, during and after his
command; Stuyvesant managed to clean it up
considerably.

One of the ironies attached to Stuyvesant was the fact
that though he was an ex-soldier himself, he managed to
succeed where the past governors failed in keeping the
peace in the colony. Not just with the many different
European settlements in New Amsterdam but with the
many different Native American tribes as well.
However; once a soldier, always a soldier and when
Peter Stuyvesant got word that a Swedish establishment
that settled in the Delaware region failed to submit to
Dutch rule, he perhaps got the itch to go to war again.
Stuyvesant mustered up two thirds of his army to march
down to Delaware to sort out the problem. Stuyvesant
left one of his Lieutenant Governors, a man named Van
Dyke (famous for his style of beard?) in charge of New
Amsterdam in his absence.

It could be argued that the whole downfall of the Dutch colony in the new world would come crashing down over one stupid incident involving a peach. Van Dyke killed a young Native American girl who was picking peaches from one of Stuyvesant's trees. This young lady happened to be the daughter of a very prominent Native American Chief. He united some of the other tribes and they attacked the much diluted Dutch colony.

Stuyvesant returned and as was furious at what he saw. Thousands of casualties on both sides, though most were natives but many of the Dutch farms were destroyed and several dozen families were taken hostage and held at high ransom. Making matters worse were rumors that the Iroquois Nation were on there way down to wipe the Dutch out completely. At the same time, the British who have been eyeballing this piece of real estate for sometime now were beginning to move in on the Dutch colony themselves.

Though Stuyvesant expelled Van Dyke, paid the ransoms for the hostages and somehow negotiated a cease-fire with the natives; word of the incident reached the Netherlands and they ordered Stuyvesant to hand the colony over to the British when they arrived. The headstrong Stuyvesant refused at first, he tore the letter to pieces and tap danced all over it with his peg leg. He locked himself in a room in Fort Amsterdam. He even stood behind a cannon and swore he would fire on the first British ship to enter the harbor but he never did. He surrendered the colony peacefully.

So the Dutch, that "acquired" this land from the Native Americans for $24.00 in junk jewelry, lost it to the British over a peach.

THE ENGLISH INVASION

In 1664 King Charles II was sitting on the throne in England and he saw how prosperous the Dutch were doing here in New York and noticed how the English colonies surrounded the Dutch in the new world. The king negotiated the trade with the Netherlands with a couple of their islands in the West Indies and sent his younger brother James, the Duke of York, to take this colony from the Dutch. After the peaceful exchange of power, the British flag was raised in the colony and it was renamed New York after James, the Duke. There were, at the time, eighteen different languages spoken in the colony, not counting the native tongues but other than the new name and the new flag, everything else pretty much stayed the same.

During British rule of New York, New Yorkers began to
evolve as a breed of their own. Prominent families
began to inter-marry and blend the influences of their
customs together. People from all over the world
became attracted to New York for many different
reasons but mostly for the money, for there were lots to
be made here. It is a geographically protected port in a
large and prosperous harbor. New York's population
began to skyrocket and the more people that came, the
more prosperous New York seemed to become.

The British during this time engaged in several wars
with the Netherlands. One of which would result in the
Dutch reclaiming New York. They even changed the
name to New Orange! Eventually the British would
reclaim it and rename it New York, for the second time
in history. That's what it has been called ever since.

REVOLUTION

By 1776, the child out grew the parent. Unwilling to meet the increasing demands of the British crown, the thirteen colonies on the east coast got together and fought the Revolutionary War. Under the father of our country, a Virginian named George Washington became General of the Continental Army and provided the leadership the colonies needed to win the war. Though New York was a huge British stronghold and most of the battles of that war fought here were lost by the Continental Army (and navy), the war was won in several other key places. In our victory, we became a brand new nation. It was a third-world nation back then but today it is the only surviving super-power of the world, the United States of America.

THE FOUNDING FATHERS OF A NEW NATION

New York City was the first capitol of this brand new
nation. It is right here where our founding fathers got
together to swore in General George Washington to be
the first president of the United States of America.
Washington's portrait is on the U.S. one dollar bill. The
portrait on the two and the ten dollar bill are other firsts
as well. Thomas Jefferson, the first Secretary of State
on the two and the first Secretary of the Treasury,
Alexander Hamilton on the ten. Jefferson, like
Washington was from Virginia and was the founder of
the Democratic-Republican Party. Hamilton, an
immigrant, founded the Federalist Party. Washington
wasn't fond of parties; he remained an Independent but
seemed to favor Hamilton.

"First in war, first in peace and first in the hearts of his countrymen."

General Henry Lee

GEORGE WASHINGTON

He's on the quarter and the one dollar bill. He is the only president we named a state after as well as our nation's capitol. He was the commander of the Continental Army, the first U.S. President but what else do we know about George Washington, the father of our country? It can probably be summed up best in one word: *leadership.*

Washington led the Continental Army for no pay and he chose to stay with his men in Valley Forge rather that sleep in a warm bed. He was one of ten Presidents who were generals and one of nine Presidents who never went to college, his formal education ended around the age of fifteen. On December 23, 1783, Washington presented himself before Congress in Annapolis, Maryland, and resigned his commission! Washington had the wisdom to give up power when he could have been crowned a king. He retired to live the quiet life as a gentleman farmer in Mount Vernon, Virginia.

Washington came out of retirement when concluded that reform was essential. He wrote to James Madison that what was needed was an energetic Constitution. Once the Constitution was approved, Washington hoped to retire again to private life but when the first presidential election was held, Washington received a vote from every elector. He remains the only President in American history to be elected by the unanimous voice of the people. He walked through a slave market in downtown Manhattan on his way to be sworn in to office and it affected him. Though he and his wife owned 300 slaves, Washington is the only founding father to have emancipated his slaves.
Washington was an early supporter of religious pluralism. On August 18, 1790 he wrote that he envisioned a country…

"…which gives bigotry no sanction, to persecution no assistance.... May the father of all mercies scatter light, and not darkness, upon our paths and make us all in our several vocations useful here, and in His own due time and way everlastingly happy."   (paraphrase)

During his service as President, Washington was a model of democracy to future presidents, setting precedents in many areas including a faith in civil, not military, rule and a focus on the will of the people above all things.

ALEXANDER HAMILTON
and
AARON BURR

Of all of our founding fathers, Alexander Hamilton was the only immigrant; he was born in the British West Indies. Hamilton was a financial genius and Washington knew this. He fought alongside Washington in many of his battles and discussed his ideas with Washington on how the country should be run. Washington remembered this and appointed Hamilton as the first secretary of the treasury in his cabinet.

At twenty-six years old, it was Hamilton who created the New York Stock Exchange down on Wall Street. He saw how all the leaders of all the merchant shipping companies got together (informally or otherwise) under a buttonwood tree on Wall Street to discuss the value of the dollar. He would soon institutionalize it as the NYSE. Hamilton also created the first bank in the country; The Bank of New York, a bank where over one third of the entire world's banking still goes on today. A prolific writer, Hamilton also co-authored the U.S. Constitution with James Madison. With his writing skills, he also started The New York Post, a tabloid newspaper back then but one of the major New York newspapers today.

Unfortunately for Hamilton, most of us hardly remember him for all the wonderful things he did for this country but instead for how tragically he died.

Aaron Burr, like Hamilton, was a great thinker. He was admitted to Princeton University at only eleven years old. Burr, like Hamilton also was a graduate of King's College, now Columbia University. Both were officers in Washington's army and both were assigned to escort the patriot, Nathan Hale and both witnesses him hung as a spy without the benefit of a trial. They hid from different fortified positions and each waited for the other to make the first move to try and rescue Hale but neither did. Neither teenager's platoon was any match for the highly disciplined British army.

After the war both worked as attorneys in New York and both were politically ambitious. Though their backgrounds may seem similar on paper, in reality the two men couldn't be further apart.

Burr was serving under President Thomas Jefferson and they didn't get along with Hamilton. For one, Hamilton was appointed where "they" had to be elected. This sharing of power seemed to confuse and irritate Burr as he was still used to the monarchy. This way of thinking even caused friction between Burr and Jefferson, so Jefferson probably did all he could to stay out of their way.

Jefferson, a southerner, wanted a democracy and Hamilton, who married into a wealthy family, was a capitalist. Hamilton thought all the power should be shared between the rich families. Burr was one of the founders of Tammany Hall, a democratic political club that gave some power and a voice to the common people. Remember, back then you had to be a land owner to have the right to vote. Burr convinced these people to "get together" in groups of three and four to buy a piece of property as so they can vote.

Hamilton made the political mistake of not getting any of his rich in-laws and their friends jobs in office where he had the opportunity to do so, so they in return failed to support his political war chest. This dashed Hamilton's hopes for the 1800 political run. When Hamilton saw his arch nemesis, Burr making political headway, he did all he could thwart Burr's efforts for the big chair. He turned to his writing skills and published a series of scathing reports that targeted Burr's personal life. Burr confronted Hamilton and demanded that he recount his articles but Hamilton refused.

So bitter enemies politically, business rivalries professionally (Burr founded The Chase Manhattan Bank) and rumors going around about their personal lives was all the fodder needed both to settle their disputes in a duel.

The two men ate breakfast together in Manhattan and actually made believe that they were friends but after the breakfast, they got down to business. They rowed their boats across the Hudson River and climbed the cliffs of Weehawken, New Jersey to settle their disputes in a duel of pistols. The cliffs of Weehawken became the choice settling grounds for duels being that they were out of the sight line of the city limits. This would be Hamilton's twenty-second duel but Burr's first. One of the ironies associated with this duel was the fact that it was Alexander Hamilton who got dueling outlawed. Just two years back he lost his son Philip in a duel so Hamilton had the law passed that outlawed dueling.

Historians can't seem to agree on how exactly the duel went down but the common majority agree that there where two shots fired in just a few seconds. Hamilton did fire first. Some say his pistol misfired, others say he fired into the air to purposely miss. Either way we look at it, it was a duel that both men lost. Hamilton was killed and Burr became a fugitive; he died a broken man in obscurity some years later somewhere on Staten Island. So that one shot, took out two of our founding fathers. The winner of that duel was Thomas Jefferson, who stayed out of that dispute and stayed on as our third President.

STEVENS INSTITUTE
OF
TECHNOLOGY

The tall building high on the bluff of Hoboken New
Jersey is the Stevens Institute of Technology. That's one
of the foremost engineering colleges in the country
named after a family of accomplished inventors and
engineers.

In 1784, the land now occupied by Stevens Institute of
Technology was purchased by a Kings College Graduate
(now Columbia University) and Revolutionary War
hero, Colonel John Stevens, who would later invent the
steam locomotive. He did that at the ripe old age of
seventy-six, which goes to show you that it's never too
late to find out what your natural genius is. This train

would take us off into a new age, an Industrial Age and we'd never look back from there.

Stevens had four sons and they all became pioneers in engineering. Robert Stevens, is known for inventing the T-rail, the form of railroad track in use today throughout the world. With his brother Edwin A. Stevens, Robert created America's first commercial railroad.

John Stevens also invented the first steam powered ocean going ferry, *The Phoenix*, in 1802 almost a full five years before Robert Fulton's Clermont, which came later in 1807. The steam engine was invented in England but used to drain out mines. Robert Fulton stole it from England and brought it to the States. Some other people tried unsuccessfully to get it working on a boat, but the boats kept sinking. Stevens success with the Phoenix was the first but for reasons not explained, it didn't seem to get a lot of attention. Stevens abandoned the idea of a steamboat and delved into where he saw a future; in trains. Fulton pressed on in the steamboats and made a huge spectacle of his mission in the Hudson River, where thousands came out to see (perhaps a disaster) his Clermont pass up every sailing ship in the river.

The rivalry between the Fulton's and the Stevens' camps would be similar to the later rivalries of the Edisons and the Teslas, where one would get the invention and the other the patent. Robert Fulton was actually successful in getting the law on his side as the first and the only provider of steam powered vessels for the next thirty years. This act may have inspired Colonel Stevens to help write the first U.S. Patent Law.

THE CHELSEA PIERS

The Chelsea Piers are what Manhattan was missing for a long period of time, a place to go and play sports. At twenty-two square miles in area and the host of the first and third largest downtowns in the world; Manhattan was becoming all work and no play. New York City leads the world in many different industries. It used to be things like commercial shipping, now its industries like book publishing and fashion, live entertainment, music, banking, finance, the list goes on. And like I said it was all work and no play until we built the Chelsea Pier's multi-level sports complex. When the shipping companies left, they took their ships with them but left their piers behind.

If you give New Yorkers enough lemons, it won't be long before we learn to make lemonade. We took the valuable space that was available on these abandoned piers so we save valuable real estate on the island. We reconstructed these piers so that we have an arena for just about any sport you can think of down here. Also inside the piers we have a sound stage where we film TV shows and movies. Television shows like NBC's Law and Order.

The movie and the entertainment business is the second biggest income producing department in New York. New York is the biggest income producing state in the union, which means that the money we make here in New York we help out the rest of the country. Our economists did some work and found that the biggest income producing department in New York State is tourism. The entertainment industry earns us three billion dollars a year but tourism earns us a whopping thirty billion dollars a year. More people visit New York City than anywhere else in the world with the possible exception of Paris.

Some of the other piers we kept like Marine Aviation, Pier 57. That's the only pier in the city that has a basement. We kept that pier and we put that to use by making it a bus depot. The MTA had it for many years and that's where city busses were dispatched from. The MTA recently sold it to a private bus company, who now rents it back to the city.

Another pier we kept was Pier 54. Pier 54 is a park now and it has a semi-circled, metal sign on the road side of

the pier that's kind of rusted out and it used to read:
White Star Lines. This pier used to belong to the famous
White Star Lines who were the owners of the R.M.S.
Titanic. Pier 54 was the pier that the Titanic was
supposed to tie up to but as most of you know, she never
made it. She hit an iceberg and sank on her maiden
voyage. The Cunard liner R.M.S. Carpathia with
Titanic's 700 or so survivors landed on one of the
Chelsea piers. The Carpathia would later be torpedoed
by a German Submarine in 1918.

Of the twenty seven ships in White Star's fleet, twenty
six of them ended in watery graves. All but one,
Titanic's sister, the R.M.S. Olympic, made it into
retirement (the scrap pile) but not without incident. The
rest of White Star's fleet is currently somewhere on the
bottom of the ocean! Many were torpedoed during
WWI.

The sinking of the Titanic would eventually put White
Star Lines out of business and then Cunard Lines took
over Pier 54. However in 1915, the R.M.S. Lusitania
left from pier 54 before being torpedoed off of the coast
of Ireland by a German submarine. This was one of the
catalysts that got us involved in WWI.

We've kept it and built a park on it but not too many
people go to it. The pier is said to be haunted by the
souls of the passenger's loved ones; who wander the pier
with the hope of meeting their nearest and dearest.

THE INTREPID

The USS Intrepid happens to be the largest sea, air and space museum on the planet. It was an active aircraft carrier commissioned after the attack on Pearl Harbor, during World War II. She was built in a Newport News, Virginia shipyard by mostly women. While the men were out fighting the war, it was the women who were at home building the ships. It took the women on the average six months long to build aircraft carriers like the Intrepid. Today, it takes men on the average only five years. The more things change, the more they stay the same.

The Intrepid also stood by for service in Korea and again in Vietnam as well and then it was used as the recovery vessel for the Mercury and Gemini missions from outer space. She rescued the astronauts; one who went on to become a US Senator, John Glenn. Then in 1976 she became obsolete; too small to handle the newer navy jets. The Intrepid is 900 feet long, that's about the size of the Titanic but it was too small for the F-14 Tomcats so the navy made her obsolete and sent her to the scrap pile. That's when Zachary Fisher stepped in. Zachary Fisher owned or managed more of the skyscrapers here in New York City than anybody else.

The Fisher Corporation festooned the Manhattan skyline with their buildings. Fisher never forgot what our veterans did for this country and he didn't want the rest of us to forget either. When he found out the navy was throwing the Intrepid in the garbage, he bought it with his own money. Fisher knew the story of the Intrepid, a great story I'll tell you later.

The Intrepid was in the fight of her life in the battle of Leyte Gulf in World War II. Japan was losing the war and desperate. They crashed two airplanes into the Intrepid, Kamikaze style; this killed one-third of the crew in the attack. A Japanese submarine also torpedoed the hull and the USS Intrepid was sinking fast. Then a typhoon hit, it was a bad storm. The captain gave up and he gave the order to *abandon ship* but the remaining crew never heard that order. The fire that killed one-third of their friends also knocked out the P.A. System, so the crew did what they were trained to do. These were largely the children of Ellis Island, for many, English was their second language. They stood at their posts; they fought the enemy, the fire and the floods. They braved the storm and they saved the ship! That's one of the reasons why she's here today.

ZACHARY FISHER

Another reason why she's here is because of Zachary Fisher. Zachary Fisher who made his fortune here in the Manhattan skyline, wanted to give some of it back. He was upset that the navy was going to put a ship with that kind of a history into a scrap pile. Fisher bought the Intrepid then went and raised the funds privately to keep it running as a museum and he donated it to us here in New York City. Even when this museum was losing millions of dollars in the first nine years it was open, Zachary Fisher refused to let it close. When his investors threatened to back out on him, he told them firmly that the men never gave up on the Intrepid and neither was he! Finally, in 1990 it started to see a profit and that is because of people like you who paid it a visit.

Zachary Fisher spent over twenty million of dollars of
his own money in veterans' causes. Fisher built
affordable housing on military installations overseas so
that people serving our country can have a decent place
to live at an affordable price. You might remember the
bombing that happened in Beirut Lebanon, on October
23rd of 1983, when a truck full of dynamite hit the
Marine barracks killing 241 service men. I remember
that well, I was there. Zachary Fisher gave a twenty-five
thousand dollar check to each of the families of those
killed in that atrocity.

In 1994; with David Rockefeller, Mr. Fisher established
the Fisher Center for Alzheimer's Research Foundation.
This funds Alzheimer's disease research with the goal of
finding a cause and cure. The Foundation operates the
Nation's largest Alzheimer's research laboratory, at The
Rockefeller University here in New York City.

Then in 1998, after a long list of civilian awards and
medals given to Mr. Fisher, President Clinton awarded
Zachary Fisher with the Presidential Medal of Freedom;
that's the highest award a civilian can win. It was his
lifetime achievement award and it's an award we should
all be inspired to go out there and achieve. President
Clinton also signed a public law that granted Mr. Fisher
an honorary veteran. Shortly after that, in June of 1999,
he passed away but we won't forget him. Zachary
Fisher left a wonderful signature behind here for us on
the Manhattan skyline and one on the USS Intrepid as

well. So when you're in the area, go over there and pay a visit to the USS Intrepid. It would be a wonderful tribute to Zachary Fisher and the veterans of this country. President G.W. Bush had a navy ship named in Zachary Fisher's honor.

THE
EMPIRE STATE BUILDING

The Empire State Building is one of the eight wonders of the modern world and it's the greatest skyscraper of them all. Lending more to its majestic allure the fact that it stands alone on Fifth Avenue as the only skyscraper in that general area as the owners of the Empire State Building planned it like that. They wanted that spot on Fifth Avenue (everybody's favorite address) and on 33rd Street. The bedrock on Fifth Avenue in that spot is only two feet below the Earth's surface. Yet if you go three blocks in either direction, you have to go down two hundred feet to get to any bedrock. But to get that coveted spot on Fifth Avenue they had to buy out the world's most expensive luxurious hotel, the Waldorf-Astoria.

The 102nd floor of Empire was originally an airport. An airport designed to take off and land airships. In 1930 this was the new way to travel across the ocean, Airship travel. Airships like the Hindenburg we're going to cross the Atlantic Ocean and dock on top of the Empire State Building. However, this idea that worked out so beautifully on paper but failed miserably in practical use. They were never able to land airships on top of the Empire State Building, it was too dangerous. They had to scrap that idea immediately. We'd have to wait for the 707 jet airplane to fly across the Atlantic. Empire was a bit ahead of its time.

Just to give you some perspective on the magnitude of the Empire State Building, think of how it took over a million ancient Egyptians over a thousand years to build the pyramids. Well it took only a little over a thousand New Yorkers a little under fourteen months to build the Empire State Building. They finished it forty-five days early, five million dollars under the budget and all in the height of the Depression. All union labor too, fare wages for all. There were steelworkers, ironworkers, sandhogs, carpenters, plumbers, electricians, tin knockers, insulators, elevator mechanics, painters and bricklayers… and many more.

The bricklayers ordered ten million bricks to build the Empire State Building. Those bricks came from the limestone quarries of Indiana, the heartland of America. That is one huge slab of Indiana real estate right in the heartland of the city! They used 9,999,999 bricks when they finished the Empire State Building. There was just one brick left over, they couldn't put it anywhere. That brick is on display in the lobby epitomizing the efficiency of the owners, managers and unions working together to get that building up, under the budget, ahead of schedule and all in the height of the Depression! This is why the Empire State Building is one of the wonders of the world. It's her management.

Unfortunately it was the height of the Depression when she went up and it was facing financial distress before she even opened her doors. The Empire State Building was too far from the financial district to compete for any of those businesses and being on 5th Avenue put it right center of the island, quite a stretch from either bridge or tunnel. So for the first couple of years it was mostly empty and nicknamed the "Empty State Building". It was facing bankruptcy and threatened with foreclosure until in 1933 when Empire had its most famous visitor still to this day. It was that 50-foot gorilla named King Kong. Everybody in the world saw this movie and they wanted to come to New York City to see what it was like to be on top of the world. The owners thought quick to convert the defunct airport on the 102nd floor into an observation deck and they charged people money to ride them to the top. Believe it or not that single stunt bailed them out of bankruptcy until the end of the Second World War came and people had money again.

The observation Deck is open every night until midnight. The Empire State Building combines our two biggest income producing departments; tourism and entertainment.

THE CHRYSLER BUILDING

Walter Chrysler would finish his skyscraper at seventy-seven stories tall and he was the first one to use stainless steel as part of its façade. He modeled that art deco look on the top of the Chrysler Building after his old Chrysler hubcaps of the 1920's. This is why the Chrysler Building is said to be the most beautiful skyscraper of them all. For reasons I'll never understand, people confuse his building with the Empire State Building. You can clearly see they're radically different in size, location and in style. The Chrysler Building is on 42nd Street and Lexington Avenue, opposite Grand Central Station.

The Empire State Building's owners were an eclectic bunch of millionaires. Of them were the Ford Motor

Credit Company and they wouldn't have it that the Chrysler Building was going be the tallest. So when Chrysler finished at seventy-seven stories, the Empire State Building went up to Eighty-nine stories and just to make sure they put that 222-foot antenna on top.

THE TRUMP BUILDING

Canal Street is called such because, strangely enough, it used to be a canal. It separated the bedrock part of the island from the swampy marshlands in lower Midtown. In the 1800s the city filled it in and now we have a street over here called Canal Street. Below Canal Street in Manhattan becomes a logistical nightmare, you don't use the up/down back and forth grid that we have in midtown for streets and avenues. Down here we use the old horse paths. The streets intertwine with the avenues and it's like a big spaghetti maze down here. If you come down below Canal Street, you're going to need a map.

Downtown Manhattan is where the bedrock gets closer to the surface again as you can tell; this is where more of the skyscrapers are. The biggest skyscraper down here is the tall on with the bright green roof top that was simply called "FORTY WALL STREET" when it was completed in 1930 but has since been named "THE TRUMP BUILDING".

In 1930 after just eleven months of construction, the seventy story skyscraper called; Bank of Manhattan Trust Building was completed. It finished first in a two way race against The Chrysler Building and was thought to be two feet taller as well. However when The Chrysler Building added her steel façade, her true height rose up to seventy-seven stories and thus Chrysler became the tallest building in the world. So for a few short weeks between April and May in 1930, The BMT Building at 40 Wall Street was the tallest building in the world.

The building sat mostly vacant for many years; the owners of the building weren't on speaking terms with the landowners, the few tenants that remained were said to be well behind on their rents and there were a number of mechanical liens on the building from contractors who weren't paid. In short, one of the tallest buildings in the third largest downtown in the world became largely ignored by most of the people that passed by her each day; except for one, Donald Trump.

DONALD TRUMP

Donald Trump was born in Queens, New York, the son of Fred Trump, a real estate developer himself. Fred Trump himself had no interest in developing in Manhattan, he saw it way over priced for anybody's budget but when Donald came of age; that was all he wanted. Before Donald was thirty years old he had already put together some of the most creative real estate deals the city has ever seen. He quickly became known as one of the city's top developers earning himself the nickname "The Donald".

Where Donald Trump saw a problem, he offered a solution and the Trump Building at 40 Wall Street became a Class "A" Trump deal. Trump managed to "acquire" the building for an unthinkable $1,000,000 (one-million dollars) in 1996. He then made deals with the contractors who had liens on the building to "forgive" them as Trump used those contractors for the renovations! Today, this very same building is said to be worth over $300,000,000! That's Donald Trump.

It's said that the skyscrapers that we have here take the place of egos in New York City. Remember that every major corporation, business, bank and company owns one. Sometimes their egos get in the way; they build or buy the biggest skyscraper that they could find and then they go bankrupt shortly afterwards, so they have to sell. The names of these skyscrapers change too fast for me to keep up with, but some of them are a constant like the Empire State Building or the Chrysler Building but my favorite building on the whole island is the Woolworth Building.

THE WOOLWORTH BUILDING

The Woolworth Building is a gothic looking building with the green copper top on it that may look a little bit like a church. In fact the nickname of the Woolworth Building is the *cathedral of commerce*. It's the tallest one in the middle of downtown Manhattan at 60 stories tall; but it was the tallest building in the world in 1912.

F.W. Woolworth's father told him that he'd never make money in nickel and dime stores. Well in 1912 he had enough of those nickels and dimes to put together thirteen and a half million dollars cash and build the tallest building in the world. At sixty stories tall, F.W. took residency in the penthouse on the top floor, where nobody ever looked down on him again. This was not only the tallest building in the world until Chrysler and Empire went up; it was the only skyscraper on this island paid for ENTIRELY in cash!

* In June of 2006, the Hearst Building near Columbus Circle, when finished will be the only other exception.

THE WORLD TRADE CENTER

The Twin Towers were 110 stories each, and each one had its own zip code. 10048 and 10049 no longer exist; I think most of you know why. The Twin Towers were 200 feet by 200 feet. That's an area of one square acre per floor per tower. The towers stood almost a third of a mile high, personifying the Manhattan skyline, in fact if you were to go to the top of the northern tower, you could have stood on top of the highest man-made observation deck on the planet. You could see nearly a hundred miles in each direction and at the same time, made eye contact with well over 25 million different people. But more than this, you would have seen where the dreams of two of our founding fathers; Thomas Jefferson's democracy and Alexander Hamilton's capitalism would have collided and coexisted in a city where people come from all over the world to have their dreams collide and coexist with one another and nobody would have ever questioned their race, creed, color, religion...

Then on the morning of September 11th, 2001 two hijacked airplanes would come out of the sky and slam into each of these towers, where shortly afterwards the towers would collapse, killing nearly three thousand people. Of the three thousand people killed, they were from over one hundred different countries. There were over 300 different languages and dialects spoken between those towers. They estimate that there were 50,000 people in those towers at the time the planes hit. I actually had three of my younger brothers in the towers; they managed to get out. But many of our family members, friends and a whole lot of familiar faces we passed on the street each day weren't so lucky. In fact they tell us, every person in America knew at least one person, who knew at least one person that worked in those towers.

To give a perspective on some of the numbers; the towers had collapsed and left a pile of rubble over twenty-six stories high. That's a pile higher than most of the skyscrapers in the world today. Though we had help from an international fire department where firefighters from all over the world responded, the fires burned for ninety-nine days before they could get them all out. We lost more jobs linked to the towers than there are people in the entire city of Atlanta, Georgia and more square footage than in the entire city of Cincinnati, Ohio.

The all glass atrium called the Winter Garden and the buildings around it with the green copper tops still badly stained black with ashes from burning jet fuel, surround the sight now known to the world as ground zero.

In fact it was right here where Henry Hudson came up the River for the first time in 1609, he looked straight ahead and saw the river bend over the horizon and he thought he found his Northwest Passage. Hudson was so excited, that he wrote down in his log book: *This will be the day that alters history*! He circled the date. That date was September 11, 1609.

On a more serious note, people also ask me what we on the Circleline were doing on 9/11, when the planes hit the towers. The first plane hit the first tower at 8:45 or thereabouts. It was too early to send any boats out on the river; our first trip wasn't until 9:30. At 8:45 am most of us were at work that day or on our way to work. We were getting our first ship ready for the cruise and then the first plane hit the tower. After the second plane hit the other tower we (like most everybody else) knew there was a serious problem.

We called up the city and we told them to send passengers our way. We instantly converted our tour boats into ferry boats and in the next four hours, we took 60,000 plus people off the island of Manhattan to safer places in New Jersey. Other ferry companies followed and did the same thing. Even tugboats that were working in the harbor put their barges on buoys out on the river and came in here and took people on their tugboats. It took the entire commercial fleet of New York City less than four hours to clear off the island of Manhattan. We did this without incident and then they shut the harbor down that afternoon.

It is here that I want to say on behalf of all of us here in New York City that we want to especially thank everybody that gave money to those fundraisers and tell you that you have helped us out in a very big way. Your money got to us in the form of a benefit and it really helped. I'd also like to thank those people that volunteered for those many different organizations who contributed to the relief after September 11th. You all showed the world what America was really all about.

THE COLGATE CLOCK

Across the Hudson River on the bank of Jersey City, New Jersey, you'll see the largest single faced clock on the planet. It's called the Colgate Palmolive factory clock and it's over fifty feet in diameter. If the arms where strong enough, twenty-two full grown men, six feet tall can stand across the hands of that clock at nine fifteen; shoulder to shoulder.

The clock came here in 1927, the same year as the Holland Tunnel and has seen a lot of things in this harbor. Like the stock market crash on black Tuesday in October of 1929. It seen thousands of GIs returning home on the Queen Mary, cheering their victory in WWII and it has seen the attacks on the entire free world

on September 11, 2001. This clock has seen many
things in the years in between as well. Colgate moved
their factory away years ago but this clock is a landmark
now and architecture laws on this clock will keep it in
this harbor here forever. This clock will see many
things in the years to come. It is a clock that will out
live us all and why not... it has the time!

HOLOCAUST MEMORIALS

There are some more buildings in Lower Manhattan
worth mention here. There is a building on the outskirts
of Battery Park City that's not very tall and almost on the
river's edge. It's a six-sided structure that has a pyramid
shaped top to it. This is the New York Museum of
Jewish Heritage. It's a Holocaust Memorial, dedicated
to all the Jews who were killed in the holocaust of
Europe during WWII. The six-sided footprint represents
the Star of David and the six windows on each side
represent the six million who were killed during the
holocaust. A lot of thought went into the symbolism
which was designed and built by a couple of Irish
architects, Gavin and Roach.

Ironically enough, if you go inland just a couple of yards, you'll find the *Potato Famine* monument that Jewish architects and artist Brian Tolle built in honor the Irish holocaust of the 1840s! So you can see that's how we get along here in New York City. We live so close to each other everybody gets cross-cultured, colliding and co-existing.

Outside of Dublin, we are the largest Irish city in the world and if you count Long Island, we're the largest Jewish city in the world as well. According to those standards, we are the largest Greek, Italian and Norwegian cities while you're at it. 70,000+ Chinese in our Chinatown gives us the largest Chinese population in America. We also have another Chinatown in the Borough of Queens. Almost one-third of the people living in New York City are of Hispanic descent and there are more African-Americans here in New York City than that of the entire population of Chicago, the third biggest city in America. But more than all of this combined is the fact that 48% of us, almost half of the people in New York City right now were born in another country! That is what makes us the richest, most ethnically diverse, cultural melting pot on the planet and other than The Twin Towers, I don't think anything exemplifies that better than Ellis Island.

"...the policy or advantage of [immigration] taking place in a body (I mean the settling of them in a body) may be much questioned; for, by so doing, they retain the language, habits, and principles (good or bad) which they bring with them. Whereas by an intermixture with our people, they, or their descendants, get assimilated to our customs, measures, and laws: in a word, soon become one people."

...George Washington

ELLIS ISLAND AND IMMIGRATION

Ellis Island is the island across the Hudson River, closer to the shores of New Jersey in New York's Great Upper Bay. It's got a castle on it with four turrets and a water tower. South of Ellis Island is Liberty Island where the Statue of Liberty stands and just north of Ellis Island, we have this building it kind of looks like a chapel. Though many people confuse this building for Ellis Island, upon closer inspection you will notice that it isn't an island but part of the mainland of New Jersey. By the way, all the islands in the harbor belong to the State of New York except for two, Ellis Island and Liberty Island. However they do not belong to New Jersey either, those two islands belong to the United States federal government.

This train station is no longer in use today, now it is a park. When it was open, it used to facilitate immigrants. Trains used to leave here twenty-four hours a day and seven days a week, and take the immigrants out to all the major cities in America. America was a new nation and a new nation needed people, lots of people. America needed to expand our cities so we opened up our doors to the world and welcomed people in from all over to our country. We needed cities and railroads and bridges and tunnels and… and… and… dreams and ideas and everything else a new nation needs. Now, one out of four immigrants stayed here in New York City, that's how we got so big so fast. The rest got on trains at this station right here and went out to the rest of America.

Could all the different peoples of the world live together in one place? America would soon become the human laboratory of social and economic sciences. But before any of those people got that lucky, they had to pass through the rigorous entrance exams of Ellis Island, which always struck a chord of fear in the hearts of people coming into this new world.

The island is named after a man named Samuel Ellis. Ellis came over here when the British had the colony and made himself a fortune in the fish market. He bought this island as private property but when the revolution broke out… Mr. Ellis sided with the British.

101

Well, he hid on the island for the duration of the war,
long story short, the war ends… and Mr. Ellis got the
message that he better get out of town. And so he did,
he was fine with that, he hated America anyway. He left
in such haste, that he leased this island to the U.S.
government for only ten dollars per year.

Over the next hundred years or so, this island was used it
for a number of different things. It was an army fort
where we hung pirates, a P.O.W. camp during the Civil
War and for many years after that, an ammunition depot.

Then on January first in 1892, the doors would open up
to the largest immigration facility on the planet and
welcomed in the largest wave of mass migration in all
human history. It is estimated that sixteen million
people come through these doors in the years it's open.
This tells us, in a twisted piece of irony, that sixteen
million people dying to get into this country will now
and forever in time have their names linked to the one
man who couldn't wait to get out! Samuel Ellis, we
never changed the name.

Try and imagine saving every cent you earn for two
whole years, then selling everything you own, that you
can't carry. That's how much money a ticket cost to get
on a boat, cross a wide and angry ocean and land on a
new continent in a new country only to start your whole
life all over again… from the very bottom of course.

You were crammed into the hulls of these ships with up to 1000 people or more sharing only two bathrooms. Your ration was a pint of water per day; you had to bring your own food. They told you that the ride would take two weeks when in all reality most of these ships got lost for months at a time. In fact, quite a few never made it. The ride over the rough Atlantic made the crammed and starved immigrants so sick that many prayed the ships would go down in the night, just to take them out of their misery. As a result, quite a few of those ships never made it; the Titanic was just one example.

For the ones who were fortunate enough to make it, they got to an island that was always crowded. An island designed to handle 5,000 immigrants a day when, in it's hey day it had to handle twice that or more. This may have required your ship to wait out in the harbor, at anchor, yet a couple of more days. Would those supplies last?

Then they finally called your ship's name and it ferried into the slip. First, they threw all your personal baggage on the lawn. For the first time you were separated from the last of the things you owned. Remember, these were the things that you held so dear that, as bad as you needed the money, you refused to sell. You walked into the building never sure if you were to see them again.

The process started on the top floor and you worked your way down. Your first order was to run up the three

flights of stairs and run you better had. You may not
have realized this but there were inspectors under the
stairs watching you. If they noticed anyone limping a
little bit or huffing and puffing a little too much, they
would come over to you with a piece of chalk and mark
a spot on your coat. That was a signal for a doctor to
take a closer look at you. Needless to say, you did NOT
want this unnecessary attention.

Italians would get a different chalk mark altogether.
Italy was the last country to come up with passports, so
the first few waves of Italian immigrants had no
paperwork. Inspectors would systematically pull them
out of the line and with that piece of chalk, in big bold
letters, they wrote the three letters W.O.P. It stood for,
without papers. You understand that this was often the
only jacket or shirt-coat they owned. This mark would
stay on their jackets as they arrived into their Italian
settlements like Little Italy, and everyone knew who the
new people were. They knew who to pick on.

For the Italians as well as the rest of everybody, the
average stay on the island was eight hours. Eight hours
of waiting on long and aggravating lines just to be
pushed and shoved from room to room. Prodded, poked
and probed in various stages of undress. You were also
asked a series of questions in English that you had better
answer in English. And at the end of it all, after eight
long and humiliating hours, you made it to the bottom
floor. You then stood in front of one final inspector who
you never seen before in your life. Yet he had less than

thirty seconds to look down his nose at you and decide whether or not he thought you were good enough to make it here in this country.

Ninety-eight percent of the time he let you in. Less than two percent were sent away. Where to? Well that wasn't our problem. But here is a hint: those ships were going back to Europe empty. But for many, going back was not an option. They checked out on Ellis Island; there are over 600 recorded suicides attached to the island. This all contributes to the island's nickname, "the island of tears." Those were tears of joy for many but tears of sorrow for quite a few.

It is said that one in five of us living in America today can trace at least one relative that went through Ellis Island. Now if that isn't you, you may recognize some of the 16,000,000 names; like comedian and entertainer of our troops, Bob Hope. He made it to 100 years old. Another comedian named Milton Berle made it to ninety-seven. Musical composer Irving Berlin, composed *God Bless America* and thousands of other popular songs, made it to 101. Broadway lyricist, Yip Harburg wrote hundreds of tunes including the most famous sung song ever, *"Somewhere Over the Rainbow."*

So did movie stars Cary Grant, Rudolph Valentino and the guy who played Count Dracula, Bela Lugosi on stage and on the big screen. The greatest performer of all time, even to this day; the magician, Harry Houdini, who did many of his shows right here in New Yorh City. There was award winning publisher Joseph Pulitzer and science fiction writer Isaac Asimov. From Ireland came Boy's Town leader Father Flannagan. Athletes; there was bodybuilder Charles Atlas and football hall-of-famer, Knute Rockne. The guy who split the atom, Albert Einstein, as well as the guys who split a lot of heads, Albert Anastasia and Lucky Luciano.

Then there was the ninety pound human skeleton, hiding from the Nazis in the mountains of Abruzzi Italy. He came through here, a virtual human skeleton but in 1959, he out lifted the strongest man in the world. He went on to become a championship wrestler and sold out our Madison Square Garden more times than anyone in history. He's known as the living legend, Bruno Sammartino!

They all came through here, the good, the bad and the ugly. America called them and they came, most of them coming from absolutely nothing and for some, even less. They followed their souls, embraced the indomitable American spirit and with wills of iron, shattered many obstacles and reached it to the top of their game. Each of those sixteen million helped make us who we are today, the only surviving super-power and they got their start right on the island of tears, as the children of Ellis Island.

"Give me your tired, your poor, your huddled masses yearning to breathe free ..."

Emma Lazarus

THE STATUE OF LIBERTY

When the immigrants passed through the front door to America (The Giovanni Da Verrazano's Strait) they got to look up at one of the most poetically perfect statues on the planet. One can only imagine the silence, the tears and the overwhelming sense of joy that must have passed through them as they stared, jaws agape at this marvel of the world. She is the tallest statue in the world to date; if you count the height of the lady and the pedestal, she stands 305 feet tall. She's the most photographed lady in the world and one of the most popular and recognized icons of freedom of the modern world. Her full name is, *The Statue of Liberty Enlightening the World*, or as we just call her here in America... the Statue of Liberty.

She was given to us by the people of France, not the
government. The people of France raised their own
money and they hired a famous French sculptor,
Frederic-Auguste Bartholdi to do the statue. Bartholdi
was so happy to do the statue he actually took the face of
his mother, Charlotte and then put it over the body of his
mistress, Jeanette.

Bartholdi used Norwegian copper as thick as two
American pennies. He and his crew pounded out this
statue that most of you know is hollow. It wouldn't be
able to stand up to the high winds of the harbor if it
wasn't for an engineer named Gustave Eiffel, who went
on to build the Eiffel Tower. He did the lady's skeleton
(the framework) out of iron and steel. But it was
Bartholdi who put that torch in her right hand, obviously
the torch symbolizes freedom. Not so obvious, in the
left hand, is the most misunderstood piece of the statue.
It is a keystone. You will notice the top two corners are
notched out. A keystone is symbolic to democracy, as
are the Grecian, Athenian robes she's dressed in; Athens,
Greece is the birth of modern democracy. The crown on
her head has seven spikes; seven points in the septagram
or the star of Elven. That is for the unity of all peoples.
There's also one spike for each continent on the planet;
people are welcome from all over the world to America.
There are twenty-four windows in the crown of her head
named after the most precious jewels in the world;
Diamond, emerald, ruby, sapphire… this symbolizes the
gifts or the talents that people to America. And the

symbolism goes on… Look at that stern look in here eye; that's the county's slogan, "Don't tread on me".

What you now know is that the French people built the statue, but the American people built the pedestal. This entire project was a joint effort between the two countries. Remember that there were no government monies involved on either end of the ocean whatsoever. Award-winning publisher Joseph Pulitzer came up with a number of different fundraisers. Of them was a poetry contest where a Jewish girl from Manhattan; native New Yorker, Emma Lazarus, wrote that award-winning poem, The New Colossus.

"Give me your tired, your poor, your huddled masses yearning to breathe free, The wretched refuse of your teaming shore. Send those, the homeless, temptest tossed to me, I lift my lamp beside the golden door…"

THE VERRAZANO-NARROW'S BRIDGE

The Giovanni Da Verrazano-Narrows Strait is another one of the gifts we got from Mother Nature. The largest harbor of the world, over 1000 miles of water front property and yet the only way to directly access the Atlantic Ocean is that one mile strait. This made us impervious to invading navies, storms at sea and rising currents. Because of that Strait, the Hudson River is actually below sea level.

Now for years, the navy's admirals were arguing with the city officials not to build a bridge between Brooklyn and Staten Island. Such a bridge over the gateway to harbor could possibly compromise the security that

Mother Nature's geography has naturally gifted the New York harbor with. A bridge over the front door to America would become too sweet of a target for anyone wishing to harm America. Simply put if that bridge is attacked, it could collapse into the harbor and serve as a blockade. All the ships in all of our navy yards would never be able to get out to the ocean; they would be stuck and rendered virtually useless at their moorings until the strait was cleared of the bridge debris. This could take months and in the Atomic Age, that is a very long time!

The navy instead argued that we should build a tunnel. However a tunnel would present a set of two different problems that stem into the same one. Money! The water in the Verrazano-Narrows Strait is deeper than the Hudson River by the Lincoln and Holland tunnels. Naturally, the deeper the water is, the heavier the water over the tunnel becomes. The heavier it becomes, the further down you need to dig for a tunnel. The further down you need to dig, the longer you have to make the tunnel and the longer that you make the tunnel, the more expensive it becomes. Also, tunnels only hold four lanes of traffic, two in each direction. If you want a wider tunnel, you have to dig down even deeper. If you dig deeper, you will have to make the tunnel even longer. Get the point? It is very similar to "rocket science". A rocket ready to blast off into space needs a certain amount of fuel to, say, get to the moon. Now if you want a similar rocket to go to, say, planet Mars; you are going to need a lot more fuel. But the more fuel you

111

use, the heavier the rocket becomes and the more
unlikely it is that the rocket will blast off. It would take
a really smart "rocket scientist" to optimize the fuel.
Similar to the tunnel situation; with only four or say
even six lanes of traffic charging a modest or even
expensive toll would take too long to recover its costs.

Now a bridge? A bridge is not only much cheaper to
build but it can host (at least in this case) twelve lanes of
traffic! A modest toll and this bridge can recover its
costs well within its lifetime.

Because of the huge shipping industry of its day, this
bridge would need to cover the span between Brooklyn
and Staten Island uninterrupted and take the title of
longest suspension bridge from the world famous
"Golden Gate Bridge" in San Francisco by about sixty
feet. Unlike the Holland Tunnel and the Brooklyn
Bridge where we credit the head engineers for their
brilliance, the man who seems to overshadow the
engineers of this bridge was the same man who was in
some way largely responsible for many of the city's
5,000+ bridges and most of our tunnels, beaches, parks,
roads and highways. This man was quite possibly the
most despotic autocrat the city has ever known. His
name was Robert Moses. The genius of Robert Moses
went unrivaled but for a few of his day. It's said that
Robert Moses had the unique ability to portend common
trends before they happened. Perhaps he saw how the
city's baby-boomers who toiled at their jobs in the city
all day and returned home to their homes in the suburbs

on Long Island by night, were just about ready to retire. And just where do most New Yorkers retire to? The sixth borough of New York, of course; Florida! And a great bridge over the Verrazano-Narrows Strait would be the missing link to get our snowbirds off of Long Island and down yet another brainchild of Mr. Moses; Interstate US 95. His highway will take you all the way to Florida without the inconvenience of Manhattan's bustling traffic.

A bridge this long presented its own set of problems. First, there was the amount of steel needed for this project. With steel, the longer you make a bridge span, the furthermore you need to stretch the steel. The further you stretch steel, the more flexible and weaker it becomes. The weaker it becomes, the more steel you need. The more steel you need, the heavier it gets. And the heavier it gets, you need... The wisdom of a "rocket scientist".

The Verrazano-Narrows Bridge was borne of Robert Moses engineering, the best and most certain of its day. One of the ways they compromised the steel dilemma was to arch the bridge towers just one degree outwards to "over compensate" for the strength of the steel. Of course, this "trick" was too good to keep secret and the sense of humor amongst the bridge engineers conspired to let out a rumor that the adjustment in the towers to accommodate the curvature of the earth! Perhaps this rumor was to "overcompensate" for Robert Moses's massive ego.

This bridge goes over the The Giovanni Da Verrazano-Narrows Strait also known as the front door to America on one side and the gateway to the rest of the world on the other. You might have recognized this bridge from the movie, *Saturday Night Fever*, with John Travolta. When we get to the Brooklyn Navy Yard, I'll talk about it more and then you'll see where it falls into place with this story.

THE HOLLAND TUNNEL

At the end of Canal Street and stretching into the Hudson River, you'll see a pier with these strange looking buildings at the end of it and an similar arrangement directly across on the New Jersey side. These buildings are the air vents for the Holland Tunnel. This would be the first tunnel of its kind but its named after its Chief Engineer, Clifford Holland, not the Providence in the Netherlands. We here in New York are very proud of our Dutch and British ancestry but it has nothing to do with this tunnel, it just happened to be the guys last name.

Clifford Milburn Holland was an actual person, he graduated from Harvard School of Engineering in 1912 and he said to his classmates that he wanted to invent something that the world would remember him by long after he was dead. So Holland got to work on this tunnel, a tunnel that in the early 1920's had to be the first one to facilitate a brand new mode of transportation known as automobiles. Cars, as most of us know, exhaust a poisonous gas, carbon monoxide. This would kill the people in the tunnel if it weren't for adequate ventilation. But how do you ventilate a tunnel nearly two miles long and at the same time, one hundred feet below a river?

The river is only about fifty feet deep. Holland's tunnel actually goes down another fifty feet under the river bed and it was built by the sandhogs; that's the union that digs tunnels, you might have read about them in Tom Kelly's novel, Payback. So the tunnel does not lay at the bottom of the river like many people think. It's a dry tunnel that goes through the rock underneath everything.

The key to the tunnel's success is its exhaust ventilators. Clifford Holland invented these exhaust vents; four of them, two on each side, eighty-seven fans each and they change the air in the tunnel every ninety seconds.

Sadly for Clifford Holland, he never lived to see his dream come true. He died before the tunnel was completed of... of all things, exhaustion. The Chinese say be careful what you wish for. Clifford Holland wanted the world to remember him by something he'd invented, invented exhaust vents and succumbed to exhaustion. The engineer that took his place also died of exhaustion. It took the third engineer to finally complete this tunnel and when he did, this was not only the first physical link of Manhattan to the mainland of America but the first tunnel of its kind and one of the eight wonders of the modern world.

THE EAST RIVER

Separating Governor's Island from Manhattan and
Brooklyn is the very swift currents of the truculent East
River. It has some of the strongest currents in all of
North America yet the East River technically is not a
river but an estuary or a title strait. That's a body of
water that connects two or more larger bodies of water.
Therefore the East River has neither origin nor
destination, it just exists. It's a title strait connecting the
Long Island Sound to the Hudson River that rushes back
and forth and seems to go nowhere fast. If the rivers of
New York City are able to reflect the land they bound;
as the Hudson's currents do for the colliding and co-
existing of cultures on Manhattan, then the East river
may reflect how the outer boroughs "bridge" their way

to Manhattan as the East River in a way bridges the Hudson to the Sound. The river's currents perhaps provide the frantic pace or the flow of the hectic bustle of the city as well.

GOVERNOR'S ISLAND

Where the Hudson River meets the East River we have a
suspicious island in the harbor known as Governor's
Island. Named this by the first Dutch governors who
stayed here on this island as they oversaw their colony
around them. When the English came and took over the
colony they used this island much in the same way their
Dutch predecessors did. Shortly after the American
Revolution, the American's fortified it and for many
years used it as an army base. They built Fort Jay in the
northern section and that round brick castle on the
Northwest corner of the island, Castle William.
William's Castle was used and run as a P.O.W. camp

from the War of 1812, all the way up to World War II.
In fact Walt Disney did some time there as an AWOL
soldier from World War I. He hated the Marines and
kept jumping the fence so they finally locked him up
there at Castle William.

In 1945 the United States Coast Guard moved onto the
island and by 1960 they took over the entire island. It
then became the largest Coast Guard base. Then in 1997
they closed it down, the island became too expensive for
their budget. Due to the loss of our commercial
shipping industry, The US Coast Guard found that this
island was far too big for it's purposes here in the
harbor. The U.S. federal government tried to sell us this
island for $500,000,000. Our Senators argued against
payment, they fought to get it returned to us as
"borrowed property". Their argument was that this was
New York's island before the military was on it, it
should be returned to us for free if they don't want it
anymore. We shouldn't have to pay for our own island.
However, the federal government stood firm on their
five-hundred million dollar demand. So we told the
Man he can take the island to Washington D.C. if he
wants.

The Man got the point and after a few years of going
back and forth, they offered the island to anyone for one
dollar! Of course there were conditions; the northern
section of the island is a historical preserved site where
architectural laws demand the maintenance of the
buildings at the owner's expense. Also the much bigger

problem with this island is that there are no bridges or tunnels that access the island. The Brooklyn Battery Tunnel, the longest tunnel in North America to date, runs under the island and one of its ventilators are on the island but it does not access any traffic to the island. The only access (so far) to the island is via a ferry service.

A number of the top real estate developers here in New York and other places had some of their own ideas of what to do with this island but all have agreed on principle over one unanimous fact. That is: the first developer on this island loses money but the second one on this island makes money. So simply put, nobody wants to be the first one on the island; they are all waiting to be the second one.

Needles to say, until we can make a physical connection to this island, the future of Governors Island is still uncertain. I always thought that it would be a great opportunity for a sports franchise to build a stadium there. Just think of all the jobs this will create. They can run ferries from any number of ports in the city, there isn't a lot of traffic on the rivers. Fans can tailgate all day on the island and after the game (as long as the ferries are dry) the fans can sober up a bit on the ferry ride back before they get to their cars.

Remember it took our government almost 100 years to figure out what to do with Ellis Island after Mr. Ellis left it. Though it was the largest immigration facility on the planet, people forgot what it was prior. Maybe we can decide what to do with Governors Island in less time. Whatever we decide, I hope we make it BIG!

THE FERRIES

In the lower part of Manhattan on the Battery Park Wall, you will see the blue and white Circleline ferries. Those are the ferries that you take to the Statue of Liberty or Ellis Island. It is best that if you want to take a ride over to Ellis or Liberty Islands that you get there early in the morning. By the afternoon, the lines to these ferries are very long and that of course could mean a long wait. Keep in mind that these islands close down at dusk, so you don't want to be stuck waiting in a long line just to be rushed through the exhibits. Get there early so you can spend as much time as you want on the islands, there is a lot to cover between the two of them. Then you head back to the city and plan the rest of your day accordingly.

STATEN ISLAND FERRY

The orange ferries in the slips on the southern end of Manhattan are the Staten Island Ferries. They started out here in 1805 by an enterprising young man from, strangely enough, Staten Island. At only fifteen years old, this teenager from a lower-middle class family got sick and tired of working on his family's farm. He saw it as a dead-end job but he figured out another way to make some money. He used to take his father's sailboat out and fill it with as many people as he could for thirty-six cents each and then he'd make that journey from Staten Island to take them to work Manhattan. The fare for the ride home was the same price. When he turned sixteen, he had enough money not only to buy his own boat, but to pay his parents off so that they could hire somebody else to take his place on their farm to do his chores. Eventually he opened up a number of different ferry routes over the years. Later on in his life, he got into the railroad business and became the most powerful railroad magnate ever and the third richest person of all time. His name was Cornelius Vanderbilt. Sixteen-year-old Vanderbilt, with his ferries, single-handedly saved Stated Island from bankruptcy.

BROOKLYN
AND
THE BROOKLYN BRIDGE

What saved Brooklyn from bankruptcy, is something hard to miss in New York City; The Brooklyn Bridge. The Brooklyn Bridge connects City Hall Manhattan to City Hall, Brooklyn.

Brooklyn, if it were a city of its own, would be the fourth largest city in the country. Its population is just over 3,000,000. Well 2,800,000+ so says the census bureau but we all know that there are a lot of people living in Brooklyn that for whatever reason don't want to be counted, so we "estimate" Brooklyn's population to be somewhere closer to the three million mark. This being said puts Brooklyn's population somewhere between Chicago and Houston. But Brooklyn can't survive as a city of its own. It needs the municipality of Manhattan. They'd have to join us as part of our city, which really wasn't possible until we built this bridge. The bridge that was thought to be impossible, The Brooklyn Bridge, is more than two and a half times longer than any other bridge ever built up to this point. Not only did it have to span the turbulent waters of the East River uninterrupted but it had to be high enough off the water so that ships in the navy yards behind it can pass under it.

But a German immigrant named John August Roebling didn't think it was impossible. He invented the very invention that makes this bridge possible, the wire rope or the steel cable. Roebling built bridges like this in Pittsburgh, Cincinnati and Niagara Falls but to do this one here in Brooklyn, his biggest obstacle wasn't the distance or the height of the bridge itself but the greedy ferry companies. He had a lot of opposition from the ferry companies here in the city that were kicking back millions of dollars to the crooked City bosses to see that this bridge would never be built. Then one day Mother Nature froze the river over solid. The ferries were stuck in their slips, rendered useless. People from Brooklyn couldn't get to work in Manhattan and were further outraged by the fact that people living on the main land of America from as far away as Pennsylvania were coming into Manhattan and taking their jobs when they lived less than 2,000 feet away yet couldn't get to work!

The Brooklynites demanded that they give Roebling a chance to build this bridge, a bridge that would take over twenty years, cost well over 100 lives and have enough steel cables no thicker than a pencil, that if you laid them all out, end-to-end, they could connect New York City to London, England.

Now, sadly, John Roebling was one of those lives lost while building this bridge. He was killed in a very suspicious accident, no doubt induced by the ferry companies, who fought the project all the way to the bitter end. But the bridge building obviously would go on. One of Roebling's younger sons would take over the operation; a Civil War hero, Colonel Washington Roebling. Washington fought in General Warren's army as an engineer who would ride up in the air in a hot air balloon and report on the location of the Confederates. He eventually married the General's sister, Emily.

Keep in mind that the Brooklyn Bridge was the deepest in the ground man has ever had to dig and the highest in the air he had to build all in the same project. The rumor is that the first man to be killed in this venture; died in the caissons below the river. He was the father of the last person killed while building this bridge, who fell from the cable structures above.

Shortly after Washington took charge of the bridge, he was injured in a very serious accident that killed many of the workers on this bridge. He was crippled with a decompression illness divers get today called, "the bends" or "caissons disease". The next bridge builder that would take over under his tutelage was his wife, the general's sister, Emily. That's right, a woman in the 1870's in charge of the single-greatest leap of civil engineering since the pyramids and it wasn't until we got a man on the moon did we achieve a feat of engineering that great again.

In 1883, Emily Warren Roebling opened up that bridge, making it one of the Eight Wonders of the World. A Bridge that connects City Hall Manhattan to City Hall Brooklyn, a bridge that also connects fathers to sons and in some ways, it connects the pyramids to the moon as well as skyscrapers to elevators.

Steel cables make bridges possible, steel cables make elevators possible, and elevators make skyscrapers possible. We here in New York City cannot expand outwards if we want to grow, we can only go up. But with skyscrapers we went up, up and away to pass up every other city to be the greatest city in the world and of all time. With the revolution of the steel cables, bells started ringing in the heads of civil engineers and inventors all over. A man named Elijah Otis invented the elevator from the steel cable. With the invention of the elevator came the birth of the skyscraper and the rest is history. You can not have a skyscraper without an elevator and you can not have an elevator without a steel cable. The steel cable was born in this bridge by the Roeblings'. We thank Mother Nature for the bedrock, the Roeblings' for the steel cables and Elijah Otis for the elevator.

On the Brooklyn side of the Brooklyn Bridge, you will find a pizza place called Grimaldi's. It is argued that this is the best pizza in the city. Ironically, on the Manhattan side of the Brooklyn Bridge, in Little Italy, you will find Lombardi's Pizza place on Spring Street. This is the first pizza place in the new world. Everybody MUST walk over the Brooklyn Bridge at least once in their lives, it is very inspiring. Here's the opportunity to get a slice of pizza on each end of the bridge and decide for yourselves which you like best. You can't go wrong. This being said; don't leave town without trying out the pizza in Tramonti on Manhattan's West 46th Street's Restaurant Row. This new kid in town is from the old school. Tramonti is the Napolitaen town in Italy that claims to be the founders of the dish we know today as pizza. Felipe, the owner, is a sixth generation pizza chef from a long line of descendents who learned the "pizza craft" from the masters back when Columbus first brought back the tomato plant to Genoa, around 1492. They make their pizza from scratch, using all natural ingredients.

As way ahead of its time as the Brooklyn Bridge was when it opened, it was obsolete on the very same day. By the fifth day it was open, tragically, up to twenty people were killed in a stampede and we realized that we needed more bridges. The bridge just north of the Brooklyn Bridge, is the Manhattan Bridge, it's the

youngest of the three. The next bridge up is the
Williamsburg Bridge. An easy way you can remember
the order of the lay out of the bridges is to just think of
that car, the BMW. Brooklyn, Manhattan, Williamsburg,
in that order and you'll never forget.

WALL STREET

We talked earlier about Alexander Hamilton's contributions to the financial status of America's economy. Now here we can discuss the financial district he set up, in particular, Wall Street.

Wall Street is home to the world famous New York Stock Exchange (NYSE). Because of the NYSE, Wall Street is the most famous street in the world. That's where all the trading goes on. In fact, Hamilton's Bank of New York is here on One Wall Street.

Trinity Church is on Wall Street too. Though skyscrapers have risen all around it, Trinity Church still stands as a significant statement of spiritual values in the heart of downtown Manhattan and still serves as a center for worship and Christian community. The famous pirate Captain Kidd was an earlier parishoner who contributed greatly to the building of the church. For many years, Trinity Church stood as the tallest building on the island and it's spire was one of the first welcoming land sights the tall sailing ships returning home would see.

One of the oldest churches in New York, its cemetery hosts the final resting places for the first Secretary of Treasury Alexander Hamilton, *"Don't give up the ship"* naval Captain James Lawrence, inventor and engineer Robert Fulton, freedom of the press advocate and printer William Bradford and amongst many others, NYU founder Albert Gallatin.

SOUTH STREET SEAPORT

The historical South Street Seaport is in lower Manhattan just past the financial district. Like most of the 1000 miles of waterfront property in New York City, the South Street Seaport is a museum. There are three tall-masted ships left there of what used to be over a thousand, a hundred years ago when we led the world in commercial shipping. Now there are just those three and they are museums, as part of the historical South Street seaport district of Manhattan. They are the Wavetree, the Peking and the lightship, Ambrose. Each of these ships has a very interesting past.

Across the river in Brooklyn, there's the Watchtower, the world headquarters for the Jehovah Witnesses and one of the largest publishing companies in the world. That's where they publish all their literature in several hundred different languages, also one of the cleanest buildings in the city.

THE FIVE POINTS

The Five Points doesn't exist anymore but if you'll follow the Brooklyn Bridge and Manhattan Bridge inland a couple of hundred yards you get to that area they used to call the Five Points. There now in its place is where the city's courthouses are.

The five points got its name for the five different streets that met in this one corner just off the site of an old collect pond that had been poorly drained. Living conditions in this area were the worst in the world. It is known as one of the most decadent slums of all time. Though the Five Points had a reputation for poverty, illnesses and infant mortality; it also served as one of the first large scale scenes for racial integration in America. It became the place where the Irish Jig met the African shuffle and we got "tap-dancing". This would be the precursor to both Jazz and Rock-and-Roll. Many blacks, whites, Catholics, Jews and immigrants from many different nations had to live in this dire poverty in their first years as new Americans. Here in the Five Points, though tensions were stressed (considering the tensions) these ethnic groups would strengthen and hold major staples in the Democrat party.

TAMMANY HALL

It is said that there has never been a time in the recorded
history of man, where there were as many brilliant
minds, geniuses and forward thinkers together, than
when our founding fathers sat down and decided to birth
a new nation. Of them were the elder
statesman/renaissance man Benjamin Franklin, our
ambassador to France and General George Washington,
the commanding officer of our troops. There was also
Thomas Jefferson who wrote the Declaration of
Independence and James Madison who authored the
U.S. Constitution along with Alexander Hamilton who
was in charge of all the money as our Treasurer. Add to
the list patriots like Patrick Henry and John Adams and a
man named Aaron Burr, who founded Tammany Hall.

UNIQUE NEW YORK

As Vice President of the United States of America under Thomas Jefferson of the Democratic-Republic party, Aaron Burr became one of the founding fathers of Tammany Hall, a political institution in New York City. It was named after a Native American, Chief (Saint) Tammany of the Lenape tribe in Pennsylvania (1683). It was an institution founded on the basis to protect the rights of Native Americans. The mention of Tammany Hall in politics today evokes images of greedy Irish politicians with bulbous noses and fat wallets sitting in a smoke filled room counting money. Yet the first (Burr), last (De Sapio) and most famous (Tweed) of Tammany Bosses were NOT Irish!

In the 1840's, Irish immigrants fleeing the Potato Famine reached the docks of New York City. With their command of the English language, fierce loyalty, wicked sense of humor, short fuses and unabashed sense to use violence at the ballot boxes made them a natural fit to run Tammany Hall. In those days the leader of Tammany Hall was William H. "Boss" Tweed, who exploited these Irish immigrants and their natural genius in politics to make Tammany Hall the most powerful political machine ever. However slick, sly, crafty and well… smarter Boss Tweed was to his peers and those who tried to prosecute him, none were as successful as the German immigrant cartoonist, Thomas Nast.

It was Nast who created the images of American icons; Santa Clause, Uncle Sam and Lady Columbia, amongst many. He was also the one who drew elephants to republicans and democrats to donkeys. But there was no sweeter target for Nast than Tammany Hall. Though many of Nast's cartoon caricatures sympathized with Native Americans and Chinese immigrants, he was openly anti Irish, anti catholic and anti democrat. He repeatedly drew the Irish as surly apes and bishops as predatory crocodiles. He always drew Tweed as fat and greedy so that is the image that stuck in the public's minds. He drew Tammany as a fierce tiger attacking decency thus the tiger became the new mascot of Tammany Hall. Though Tweed was elected to the US Senate, he eventually was taken down and jailed for corruption but Tammany Hall would survive and even flourish. Every boss from 1872 till 1949 was either Irish or Irish American. The best years of Tammany like for many people were in the 1920's, where Tammany Hall got New York Governor Al Smith nominated as the democratic presidential candidate.

After years of ups and downs, wins and losses and eventually the inevitable in-fighting, Tammany began to weaken. At the end of WWII, many of the powerful and more successful leaders fled to the suburbs leaving Tammany Hall with a future that was uncertain at best. In 1949 the new Tammany boss was the youngest boss to ever hold that position and the first non-Irish boss in over seventy-five years. He was a man we all knew as "The Bishop" Carmine De Sapio.

De Sapio was born in Lower Manhattan of Italian decent. He purposely distanced himself from organized

crime members who were eager to bridge their way into
Tammany's matrix. However this turned out to be the
least of his problems. Though De Sapio was the leader
who lowered the voting age to eighteen and it was he
who came up with the rent control laws and fair
employment practices we have today, he suffered some
crushing defeats, mostly from the federal government.

Franklin Delano Roosevelt stripped Tammany Hall of its
federal patronage then backed Fiorello LaGuardia for
mayor of New York City who beat De Sapio's
candidate. Tammany was severely weakend with this
defeat and though De Sapio rallied back by winning the
mayor and governor seats once again for Tammany, he
convinced FDR Jr. not to run against his candidate for
Attorney General. However, his mother, Eleanor
Roosevelt didn't take this well. She swore revenge on
Tammany Hall and split the democrat party with
"reformers"; largely rich limousine liberals and a new
set of voters; women! Tired of a male dominated
institution, the women of the democrat party were quick
to embrace the rantings of the six foot tall first lady and
followed her allegory all the way to the polls. This
severely diluted the democrat party and with in a few
short years, the old tiger saw young lions circling for the
kill. After De Sapio was incarcerated on trumped up
charges of conspiracy and bribery, Tammany Hall
closed their doors in their once swanky West Village
building and faded into the underground.

Tammany Hall today is no longer the formidable political force it was for many years but still thrives in local clubs throughout the city. There are no more "Bosses" who control city budgets but District Leaders who associate people with their local politicians.

The oldest, biggest and most well organized is the McManus Midtown Democratic Association on Manhattan's Westside. It was founded 1901 by Thomas McManus and has been run by the McMani for well over 100 years. Their leader today is a man with guru status the city knows affectionately as "Jim" McManus. Staffed with officers, soldiers and an endless stream of volunteers of all different races, creeds, colors and religions; they work tirelessly liason-ing the community with local politics, solving problems and the all important, getting the vote out. This multi-cultural institution in Hell's Kitchen is the future of politics, today.

"The bosom of America is open to receive not only the Opulent and respectable Stranger, but the oppressed and persecuted of all Nations and Religions; whom we shall welcome to a participation of all our rights and privileges, if by decency and propriety of conduct they appear to merit the enjoyment."

George Washington

IMMIGRANTS

When the immigrant first came over here, they had very little money left over for affordable housing. They had spent most or all of it on their tickets to get here so affordable housing was kind of non-existent. They had to scurry to live with family members who came over in advance, friends or at least people of their own kind. That's when neighborhoods started to develop like Chinatown, Little Italy and dozens of other ethnically diverse neighborhoods. These neighborhoods became crowded, very crowded and then overcrowded. There were a lot of problems with these living conditions here. Modern plumbing was non existent in those early days. People pretty much did their business in buckets and then flung it out the window. This led to the spread of many infectious and contagious diseases, like typhoid and tuberculosis. There was also a lot of crime with politically backed street gangs and other problems like the exploitation of child labor and infant mortality.

It took the efforts of one of the early reformers of the day. He was an award-winning journalist by the name of Jacob August Riis. Riis was a Danish immigrant who grew up in dire poverty himself and wanted to do something about it. Riis had a fascination with the way people lived in the slums and wrote about these areas and its conditions in numerous reports that got very little attention at first... Until he got his hands on a camera! Riis soon discovered that we as humans only retain about twenty percent of the things we hear or read but we remember 100% of the things we see.

So Riis began his crusade by taking dozens of photos, most pretty graphic in nature of the pathetic lives of the wretched souls in these squalid ghettoes. He reported on how he saw up to seven families living in one room of an apartment, can you imagine that? SEVEN FAMILIES PER ROOM! That's about twenty-five people in one apartment house. Try and imagine the smells.

Riis published his reports in a book that you can still buy it today, it's on the shelves of Barnes and Noble as we speak, it's called: _How The Other Half Lives_. To show you the power of one, Jacob Riis got his book published, and it got the attention of a very powerful politician here

in New York. He was the police commissioner at the
time but would go on to become the President of the
United States of America, Theodore Roosevelt Jr.

Together, they revamped the whole way that we build
buildings today. This is why we have occupancy laws,
and adequate space for ventilation. Buildings now had
to be built with strict plumbing and electrical codes, all
thanks to the work of Jacob Riis. They built these
bridges too; they doubled as escape routes so that people
living in these squalid ghettos of the inner city could
flee out to the suburbs and into the outer Boroughs and
Long Island.

BROOKLYN NAVY YARD

Officially, the little bay here just south of the Williamsburg Bridge is called Wallabout Bay. Unofficially it is still called the Brooklyn Navy Yard but historically this was the host of the first official penal institution in America.

This is where the British kept a dozen or so warships anchored as P.O.W. camps during the Revolutionary War. Sadly this has almost become a forgotten chapter of our history. There were over 4,000 deaths on the battlefield during our war of independence but what many people don't know is that up to three times as many; 11,700+ men many as young as thirteen years old, died of starvation, dysentery, infectious diseases, neglect and in many cases beaten to death as P.O.W.s on the hells ships of Wallabout Bay. Ships like the HMS John, the HMS Scorpion or the biggest one of all, the HMS Jersey.

The ships were over crowded with prisoners forced to live in their own filth. Escape was virtually impossible, many who tried were either swept away by the swift currents of the unforgiving East River or turned in by British sympathizers if they were lucky enough to reach the Manhattan shoreline. Although there are a few stories that reflect some feats of true courage, most of these men had a horrible ending. Each morning a British officer would throw open the deck hatch and shout down the command of: *"REBELS, TURN OUT YOUR DEAD!"* The Continental prisoners would pass up their comrades' bodies who passed away in the night to the Hessian Mercenaries who the British hired to guard the hell ships. They would then simply unceremoniously fling the corpses into the river. The British would then shout down into the hold asking if anyone would volunteer for service in the King's Army. All these men had to do was to stand up and swear their allegiance to the King and they'd be released, but very few of them ever did.

Our price of freedom did not come for free. It came on the backs of men and women greater than us. It all started in the Revolutionary War and continues on in all the wars to date. It wasn't just Americans in the hulls of those ships either; there were descendants of the first African American slaves in America who worked on building the wall down on Wall Street and French, Spanish and German mercenaries as well. When the war ended we made a mass grave at Fort Green in the Brooklyn Navy Yard, and raised a monument dedicated to these brave men. It is to date the highest point in Brooklyn, honoring the 11,700+ men who paid for our freedoms with their lives.

In 1865 shortly before he was assassinated, President Abraham Lincoln commissioned this the Brooklyn Navy Yard, where it was mostly the women who worked on the docks building the ships, the planes and the ordinance for the war effort. Women like Rosie the Riveter worked around the clock pounding on the hulls of the iron-clad submarines, the Merrimac and the Monitor. They saw service in the Civil War on opposite sides. The battleship Maine that was sank in Havana Harbor, got us into the Spanish-American War; that came out of the Brooklyn Navy Yard as well. So did what we call the book-end battleships of World War II; the battleship Arizona, the first casualty of the Japanese attack at Pearl Harbor and the battleship Missouri that the Japanese had to board and give their unconditional surrender. All those and many, many more ships came out of the Brooklyn Navy Yard as well as the steamship Niagara that laid the first trans-Atlantic cable. That got us to talk to Europe on the phone.

Then in 1965, a hundred years after its inception, the navy left town. The navy left town because we built that Verrazano-Narrows Bridge, the bridge that I told you to

remember by the Statue of Liberty. It's the longest
suspension bridge in the country; it goes right over the
only strait that goes directly to the Atlantic Ocean. This
the navy did not like; the navy doesn't like bridges
altogether. They have a hard time getting their ships
under them but they claimed that this bridge, if we were
ever attacked, would be a target and if that this bridge
was destroyed, it'll fall into the strait and serve as a
blockade. That the ships in the navy yard here and in
the rest of the harbor would never be able to get out and
defend the country, they'd be stuck here useless. So for
years, the navy admirals petitioned the city not to build a
bridge there but to the navy's protest, we built it anyway
in 1964 and so the navy left town. It was the most
expensive bridge in the world and when the navy left
town, we saw how expensive that bridge really was.

Shortly after the Navy would leave, we'd lost our
commercial shipping industry. The shipyards in the
Brooklyn Navy Yard and all along the Brooklyn
Waterfront would slowly begin to leave, they'd find
other ports down the East coast or in the Gulf of Mexico
region or where ever else they had the last of the
commercial shipping.

HOUSING

The housing projects over on Manhattan's lower
Eastside were built in the 1940's, originally designed for
the returning soldiers and sailors from WWII. Projects
are affordable city housing for low income tenants. The
first occupants awarded residencies in these projects
were the soldiers and sailors returning home from the
war. The GI's had affordable housing on this side of the
river and decent paying union jobs on the other side of
the river in Brooklyn in the shipyards. Pounding their
swords into plowshares as they say in the Bible and all
was good for about twenty years.

Then the navy left town and shortly afterwards we
would lose just about all of our commercial shipping.

All those jobs in the shipyards in Brooklyn would leave.
The GI's in the housing projects would retire and flee
out to the suburbs... or to the sixth borough of New
York... Florida!

Something happened here in the city called white flight,
the money began to leave, and the city panicked and
opened up its books to pay out welfare. That opened up
the doors for people from all over the world to come and
cash in on the welfare. This opened up a whole other
can of worms. People moved into these buildings called
squatters, and they chased out a lot of decent people. A
crime wave would sweep through, a drug epidemic, and
through the 70s and 80s and some of the 90s New York
City would fall upon some hard times. A recession
would set in because we lost our commercial shipping
industry and that was the biggest income producing
department of the day for New York. This was a
recession that the rest of the nation would feel because
the rest of the nation counts on the money that New
York makes.

Most senators go to Washington D.C. every year to tell
the capitol how much money they need to bring back to
their state to balance their budget; that's the job of the
senator, get money. This is probably why they get six
year terms with no term limits. Senators in New York
get to do something completely different. The senators
of New York go to Washington every year to tell the
capitol how much money we can give them. This just

answered the question as to why people from other States want to become senators in New York.

After we got attacked on 9/11 our Senator Hillary Clinton, got up on T.V. and she answered the question everybody wanted to know; "what can we do to help out New York?" She said, "Just come here". Because coming here to New York City, the money you spend in our community works its way through the capitol and then out back into your communities back home. That's how the economic system works, so by coming to New York City you also fulfill your patriotic obligation to this country.

About the time the 1990s rolled around New York started to change. Remember earlier how I said it only takes fifteen percent of the people to move the rest? That's just what would happen here. People from all over the world would come to New York City; changing their names, perhaps changing the spelling of their names; reinventing themselves. *"You are who you make people believe you are"*.

That's what Jack Kennedy's father, Joseph Kennedy used to say about New Yorkers. People would follow this mantra from all over the world. Everyday, people of all races, creeds, colors and religions came here from all over the world to make it big in perhaps in the entertainment industry, the second biggest income producing department or maybe work in an office in one of these major skyscrapers all those major corporations

and companies own. Maybe to become a hotshot banker
or trader in the Wall Street area or in fashion,
publishing, real estate, law or medicine. Ninety-seven
percent of all the doctors in the United States of America
get some part of their training in many of the world
famous hospitals here in New York City. Or maybe
they had some ideas of their own like opening up
restaurants or to drive cabs, paint nails, cut hair or shine
shoes.

All these people needed a place to live. Where do you
think they went? They moved into the city projects and
pushed the squatters out! They got together and made
deals with the city to buy their apartments for one dollar
but by putting up the money to refurbish the buildings
that the squatters condemned. This idea went on with
considerable success. Suddenly one building at a time,
one apartment at a time, one street at a time, the city
would begin to take itself back and reinvent itself
Alphabet City for many years, it was an open-air drug
market. Now you'll see avenues of family owned
businesses, restaurants with sidewalk cafés, round -the-
clock diners and coffee shops with local talent
performing their talents.

"You are who you make people believe you are." Look
how we live here in New York City; stacked up on top
of each other in these buildings with people from all
different corners of the world. Many came here as
complete strangers, many polar opposites but we got
together and got organized. They became their own

154

breed of people; co-op tenants. Many of these co-ops have turned into condominiums today. We get up each and every morning to run down the stairs and stuff ourselves into long iron subway trains that rush up or downtown into the first or third largest downtowns in the world. We work in offices in skyscrapers as high as they can build them, as fast as they can get them up and as many as they can build here in the first and third largest downtown in the world. For what we lack in patience we make for in tolerance and that's our character. Character is what makes New York City the greatest city in the world. That's why we have over eight million of them here.

The Irish have a saying about character: *"Fame is a vapor, riches take rings, popularity an accident, your friends will come and go. There's only one thing that endures; there's only one thing with any lasting quality and that is character"*. Think about it; your character arrives on the scene before you do and lingers on after you leave. You do it right and it sticks around a long time after you leave. So it's not just the bridges and the tunnels, it's not the skyscrapers, it's not any of the gifts from Mother Nature, it's the character that makes New York City the greatest city in the world.

New York City is the only city in the world where everybody mutinies but nobody deserts. Walk down any street here in New York City and you will find yourself in the middle of a live play with everybody around you a different character in your own show. It would be a wonderful city if anyone ever finishes it, but I doubt it ever will, because the only permanent thing in New York City is the promise of constant change. It's a city with a future comes to audition, as former mayor Ed Koch used to say.

QUEENS

Where Brooklyn ends and Queens begins we have Newtown Creek, that's the official border between the two Burroughs. Queens is the largest borough in area and has more free-standing houses of the five. It's the second most populated next to Brooklyn but he most ethnically diverse. If Queens was a city of its own, it would be number six in size, right behind Philadelphia. The Citibank Building in Queens, 58 stories tall, makes it the tallest building in New York City that's not in Manhattan. If you flew into New York City from some other part of the world, chances are that you'll land in either Kennedy Airport or LaGuardia Airport, both are in Queens. So is the U.S. Open, so were two World's Fairs. The New York Mets play baseball in Queens,

they have a stadium in Flushing called Shea Stadium.
It's the only stadium in the whole entire league named
after an attorney, William Shea.

Famous people from Queens include; Donald Trump,
Archie Bunker, of *"All In The Family"*. Both the actor.
Carol O'Connor and the character, Archie Bunker. So is
Mary Tyler Moore, the young single hip New York
woman of the 1970s. Of course jumping right into her
role, the young single hip New York woman of the
1990s, Sara Jessica Parker's, Cary Bradshaw filmed her
"Sex In The City" series right over in the Silver Cup
Studios. Singers; Tony Bennett, Woody Guthrie, Louie
Prima, Simon and Garfunkel. LL Cool J, Run DMC and
Fifty Cent are also from Queens. Actors James Caan
and Christopher Walken are from Queens, so is
Everybody Loves Raymond; Ray Romano and
everybody's favorite superhero, Spider Man.

THE UNITED NATIONS PLAZA

This is the building that looks kind of like a deck of cards standing up here on the East Side right off the East River. It's got no windows on the north or south sides of it but it's got all these bright green colored windows facing the river and the city to the west. Though it is on land in Manhattan donated to them by the Rockefellers, the United Nations complex is not considered American soil. Once you go into the U.N. you leave America, in theory. This is a very sensitive area for many people. The function and purpose of the United Nations is a hard subject or a hot topic for debates of late. It's also the brunt of jokes I can't tell anymore, I keep getting yelled at…

The U.N. is currently where 192 different countries under Secretary Ban Ki-Moon, sit around trying to solve the problems of the world.

The U.N. happens to be in one of the richest neighborhoods in the world. In fact, of the top ten richest neighborhoods on the planet, six of them are here in Manhattan. This has got to be the site of at least two of them; this is where Sutton Place and Tudor City are. Most of the people living in these neighborhoods live in some of the last free-standing homes in Manhattan. They are mostly swanky co-operative townhouses. Some of these apartments start at two to three thousand dollars per square foot. Sometimes having that kind of money just isn't enough. Choosing to live in a co-op presents another set of hurdles. Many of these co-op boards are famous for turning down people with lots of money just because… well, fame. A lot of people who can afford this kind of lifestyle are very famous people. That is just what the co-op boards DON'T want. They are quiet professionals who don't want the paparazzi or news teams in their lobbies everyday taking pictures of them. The favored criteria for admissions within these co-op boards are to be very rich but not at all famous. If you can figure out a way to make lots and lots of money and not get famous for it, you have a great shot at living in these neighborhoods. If not, there is always… The Donald!

TRUMP WORLD TOWER

The tall black building behind the U.N. is the tallest of all Donald Trump's real estate extravaganzas. Trump's World Tower at the U.N. is ninety stories tall (72 actual floors). That was the tallest all residential building on the planet when completed in 2001 at the cost of $300 million dollars. Donald Trump set it right up over there to the dismay of snooty co-op tenants in the town homes I was just discussing. They fought Trump tooth and nail to see that his building would not be built. They argued to the city that his building would block their views. Trump argued back, "What views? The views are from the Queens to Manhattan, not Manhattan to Queens!"

ROOSEVELT ISLAND

Right across from the richest neighborhoods in the
world, you have Roosevelt Island. Roosevelt Island
used to be called Blackwell's Island. The Blackwell's
bought this island from the city and built a small but
successful farm on it. The Blackwell's daughters
became the first female physicians in America!

Afterwards, the Blackwell's sold their island to the city
and the city renamed it Welfare Island. When this was
Welfare Island back in the 1800s, you didn't want to
come here. Often coming here was pretty much a one-
way ticket. Charles Dickens wrote about this in his one
of his novels, where the city had that famous lunatic
asylum. It had work houses, poor houses, maximum

security prisons and quarantine hospitals. This is where the city put people that they didn't want to deal with any more. Over the years a lot of stories started to circulate throughout the city of rumors about the horrible conditions of the island.

NELLIE BLY

Elizabeth Cochrane was born in Pennsylvania into a
fairly poor family. Her mother was left with fifteen
children to raise. Elizabeth was not the best student in
her class though she did develop a strong desire to be a
writer. At sixteen Elizabeth moved to Pittsburgh to find
work. Then one day she read an article in the local
paper entitled *What Girls Are Good For*, that in a sense
bashed women. This article would change the course of
journalism in America. Furious, Elizabeth wrote a letter
of protest to the editor, George Madden. Madden
responded and after a brief exchange commissioned
Elizabeth, who was only eighteen, to write an article on
the lives of women. Elizabeth accepted, but she used a
pseudonym: Nellie Bly. *"You are who you make people*

believe you are" and from there, Bly became one of the most famous female journalists of all time.

Madden became so impressed with her gritty style, he hired her as a full-time reporter. She often got her material by undertaking a series of undercover adventures. She worked in a Pittsburgh factory to investigate child labor, low wages and unsafe working conditions. Bly was not only interested in writing about social problems but was also willing to suggest ways that they could be solved.

Her international fame reached one of the children of Ellis Island himself, Joseph Pulitzer, of the *New York World* newspaper. Over the next few years she pioneered the idea of *investigative journalism* by writing articles on poverty, housing and labor conditions here in New York City. When the city refused to let Pulitzer's reporter investigate the rumors on Welfare Island, he hired Bly to do some of her famous undercover work. Bly feigned insanity to get herself admitted into New York's insane asylum on Welfare Island.

Bly discovered that patients were fed vermin-infested food and physically abused by the staff. The city had hired the prisoners in the jails as orderlies in the asylums and their orders were simple: *"Keep the patients quiet by any means necessary"*. This was before any watchdog groups were popular, try and imagine the abuses! She also found out that some patients were not psychologically disturbed but were suffering from some kind of a physical illness. Some had been maliciously placed there by family members.

Bly's scathing reports on the conditions of Welfare Island forced the city to shut the island down. Move the prisons and hospitals to different parts of the city and it wasn't until the 1950's when they opened this island up again.

They made Welfare Island a residential community where it is today but it wasn't until the 1970s rolled around that the city realized that the term *welfare* had negative connotations to it. Who would buy real estate on such an island named Welfare? So they changed it and renamed it after the first president of the United states of America to be born here in New York City; president Theodore Roosevelt Jr.

THEODORE ROOSEVELT JR.

Theodore Roosevelt Jr. was born on 20th St. in a
Manhattan neighborhood called Gramercy. He was a
former police commissioner in New York City, one of
our former governors of the State, a former Secretary of
the Navy and the Vice President before becoming the
President of the United States of America. Roosevelt is
also the only President so far to have won the coveted
Medal of Honor, the nation's highest award. This was
awarded to him for his heroic charge up San Juan Hill,
in a Brooks Brothers suit, during the Spanish-American
War. Unfortunately for him he didn't receive this award
until nearly eighty years after his death, in the year 2001.
Incidentally, President Roosevelt had a son named
Theodore. General Theodore Roosevelt III also won the

Medal of Honor for his heroism on Utah Beach during
the Normandy invasion during WWII. The Roosevelts
became one of the few father and son pairs who, like the
MacArthurs, won the nations highest award.

President Roosevelt had a younger brother named Elliot.
Elliot had a daughter named Eleanor. She stood at just
about six feet tall and championed many women's
causes. Eleanor married her fifth cousin, Franklin
Delano Roosevelt, the President of the United States of
America during World War II. They were from the rival
branch of Roosevelts; Democrats from Hyde Park as
Teddy's family where Republicans from Long Island.

HELL GATE

At the end of Roosevelt Island, we've got a fork in the river up ahead. You've, heard of forks in the road, we've got them in rivers too. My favorite New York Yankee: Yogi Berra used to say: *"If you see a fork in the road, take it."* I'll talk more about Yogi a little bit later on when we get to Yankee Stadium.

If we wanted to take the right fork, we would have to first go under two bridges. The First of the bridges is a suspension bridge; The Triborough Bridge, the crowning achievement of a very controversial figure that lived here in the mid-1900s. His name was Robert Moses.

The second Bridge over Hell Gate is the Hell Gate Bridge. Those of you from Australia would recognize it;

it's the same architect who did your Sidney Harbor
Bridge. Only the Hell Gate Bridge is about one-sixth
the size of the Sidney Harbor Bridge.

This area is where three different bodies of water collide
but do NOT co-exist. Not now, not since the beginning
of time and probably not ever. These three waters, the
East River, the Harlem River and the Long Island Sound
hate each other. This is where they all flow into one
area and the result is very turbulent currents. The Dutch
were the ones who named it Hell Gate because they
believed the devil lived underneath and would pull the
ships under. To make matters worse, we have sharp
rocks just above or beneath the surface, in those rough
currents that tore the hulls of many ships through and
through.

We lost a lot of ships in that area including a British
payroll ship that was carrying hundreds of millions of
dollars of gold and silver bullion. She sank and the gold
was scattered and lost on the bottom. Rumors have it
that it is still there but it is unobtainable. The tides are
too swift and the waters are too cold and dark. Every
treasure hunter group in the world is familiar with the
saga of the HMS Hussar in Hell Gate but few dare to
take the dive. Every once-in-awhile an expedition team
of divers go down to look, but only a few were able to
come up again and with very little gold. We will have to
wait for better technology to pursue the riches of Hell
Gate. But plans are hatching...

"Robert Moses put the mayor in Gracie Mansion, put the U N on the East River, put Pavoratti in Lincoln Center, the Mets in Shea Stadium and chased the Dodgers to Los Angeles."

Tim Hollon

ROBERT MOSES

Robert Moses who we mentioned earlier could be possibly the most despotic autocrat the city ever knew. But he is also responsible for most of our bridges and tunnels, beaches and parks and roads and highways. In fact every foot of every highway in North America can be traced right back to Robert Moses or one of his acolytes. With the Triborough Bridge, Robert Moses did for us what Mother Nature couldn't do since the beginning of time; connected three of our boroughs. His bridge connects Queens to the Bronx, and the Bronx to Manhattan.

Robert Moses, a city planner who wore many hats in his day, was at one time (amongst many other titles) our

Parks Commissioner. He was the guy that we say that tried to *"Los Angelize"* Manhattan with his highways. People came from all over the world to see what Robert Moses was doing with his roads. Did you know that this king of the Road never himself had a driver's license? Robert Moses was afraid to drive, so he always had a chauffer. He took his road test one day but failed it miserable and was too embarrassed to go back to re-take it. But the controversy with Robert Moses really blossomed when he got into public housing.

THE GENERAL SLOCUM

Another ship we lost in the vicious Hell Gate tides was the General Slocum on June 14th in 1904. This was the third worst sea disaster of all time in America's history. An estimate of 1,100 people went down on that boat, making it the largest loss of life in a single event in New York City up until the attacks of 9/11.

Since her launch in 1891, The *General Slocum* had been cursed. She ran aground off Rockaway one night with almost 5,000 passengers on board. She hit a sand bar so hard the electrical generator went out and hundreds of passengers were injured in the panic. In August 1894, she ran aground again this time off Coney Island. In September, she collided with a tugboat in the East River and sustained substantial damage. In July 1898 she

collided again, this time with the *Amelia* near The
Battery off of lower Manahttan. Then in August of
1901, she was carrying what was described as 900
intoxicated Anarchists. Some of the passengers started a
riot and attempted to take control of the vessel from the
captain. The crew fought back and the captain docked at
the police pier where 17 men were arrested by the
police.

On June 14, 1904, the ship had been chartered by the St.
Mark's Evangelical Lutheran Church in the German
district of Manhattan called *Kliendeutchland* (Little
Germany). This was the 17th annual tradition for the
group. Over 1,300 passengers, mostly women and
children, boarded the *General Slocum*. It was to sail up
the East River to a picnic site on Long Island.

Somewhere in the East River, a fire started in a storage
compartment below decks. The ship's lifeboats and life
preservers were useless. The life preservers were rotten
and fell apart in the passenger's hands and the lifeboats
were tied up and inaccessible. Desperate mothers placed
life jackets on their children and tossed them into the
water, only to watch in horror as their children sank due
to the condition of the jackets. Remember, the
population of the boat consisted mainly of women and
children, most of whom could not swim. Some
passengers attempted to jump into the river, but the
fashion of the day made swimming impossible. Women
wore ankle length "hobble skirts" which restricted their
leg movement.

The Captain, William Van Schaick, made some very poor choices. He decided to continue his course rather than stop at a nearby landing. He later explained that he didn't want the fire to spread onto land! By the time the *General Slocum* was beached at North Brother Island, just off the Bronx shore, an estimated 1,100 passengers had been killed either by the fire or drowning. Van Schaick and the rest of his crew suffered no fatalities but he lost sight in one of his eyes from the fire.

There were many acts of heroism among the passengers, witnesses, and emergency personnel that day. The staff as well as some of the patients from the hospital on North Brother Island formed human chains and pulled victims from the water.

This disaster is why the US Coast Guard enforces strickt regulations like an exact head count of all passengers and mandatory inspections of the emergency equipment on all passenger ships. The remains of the *General Slocum* were recovered and converted into a barge, which eventually sank in a storm in 1911.

RIKERS ISLAND

If you continue on into the East River, you will eventually find Riker's Island, the largest maximum security prison in the world built on a man-made island made up of garbage and waste material!

16,000 inmates are incarcerated on Riker's Island with 130,000 prisoners that pass through their each year and onto other prisons. I really didn't know what that number meant until one day when I asked a Corrections Officer I met on one of my tours who worked there. He told me that most State prisons have two or three thousand inmates. Now picture more than half of Yankee Stadium!

Eventually the East River spills out into the Long Island Sound which will take you right out into the Atlantic Ocean.

GRACIE MANSION

At the end of Manhattan on East End Avenue and 88th St. you can see a yellow house where there is usually a white tent on the back lawn. This is Gracie Mansion, the former home of Archibald Gracie who in 1912 refused to pay his income taxes so the city took his house. It is one of the last free-standing houses in Manhattan and since 1945 it is now the home of the mayors elect of New York City.

Ironically the first mayor to be awarded residency in Gracie Mansion was Fiorello LaGuardia, the man we named one of our airports after. Mayor LaGuardia elected to reside in his modest one-bedroom apartment in the city. He though that with all the cut-backs he was asking people to make during the depression; it would look too presumptuous for him to live in a mansion. Yet, the mayor we have today doesn't live here either. Our mayor now, is the multi-billionaire, Mike Bloomberg. Bloomberg also resides in his former residence. The mayor we had before him, Rudy Giuliani, one of the heroes of 9/11 and who had done a lot to shape up the city even before 9/11; couldn't live there in his last two years as mayor. His wife had thrown him out! As a result, Gracie Mansion has been empty for the past several years but it's open up to the general public seven days a week. You can come here any time you want, for a visit.

THE LITTLE FLOWER

Some will say that the first mayor to live in Gracie mansion was the greatest mayor we ever had. This will be hard to argue. Fiorello LaGuardia was born here in New York City from a Jewish mother and a catholic turned Athiest father. He was raised as a Presbyterian but not in New York City. His father was a musician in the army so they traveled around the mid west a lot, but stayed in Arizona most of the time. This would explain Mayor LaGuardia'a accent, or lack-there-of.

Besides being a talented musician himself (he on occasion conducted orchestras) he developed a fondness for foreign languages and learned seven of them. He worked as an interpreter on Ellis Island while attending

179

New York University Law School at night. His interest in politics got him elected to congress as a republican, where he represented what is now called Spanish Harlem. While there, he took time out to volunteer for the service during World War I. He attained the rank of Major in the Aviation section of the Signal Corps and survived a plane crash. Upon returning to congress, he found his true life dream would be to become the mayor of New York City.

He resigned from congress to run for mayor but the Republicans thought his ideas were too radical so they turned their backs on him. This was also the same time his wife and baby died. La Guardia slipped into major depression but pulled himself together to run for congress again and won. He spent ten more years in congress where he got many laws passed that favored the poor and working class; one of them was the minimum wage law we have today.

His time came in 1934 when he ran for the mayor of New York City again and this time he won. LaGuardia took the oath of office and then over the radio, he repeated the pledge that the young men of ancient Athens took when they were old enough to become citizens:

"We will strive to transmit this city not less but better and more beautiful than it was transmitted to us."

This promise was delivered, largely with the help of a man we knew as Robert Moses. LaGuardia made the high rate of unemployment during the depression his top priority. He did away with a lot of "no-show" and "cushy" jobs that were bleeding the city's payroll and himself, cut his own salary by over $8,000 and refused to live in Gracie Mansion (for his first term). This gave him a budget to show President Roosevelt so that he could get funding ($23,000,000) for public works projects. Here he would shake hands with Robert Moses to build bridges, tunnels, subways, beaches, parks and highways all over the city. Many of the unemployed were put to work sprucing up the city.

LaGuardia was re-elected again in 1937 for the wonderful job he did cleaning up the city, not just on the outside but just as importantly on the inside as well. He had successfully prosecuted several major crime bosses who amassed untold power and influence during prohibition. But the one thing the flying mayor wanted more than anything was an airport within the city limits.

The closet airport New Yorkers used was across the river in Newark, New Jersey. Once, when the mayor's flight landed, he refused to get off the plane. He waved his ticket in the faces of the authorities and demanded to be taken to New York as that was what his ticket clearly read. The flustered airline promptly flew the feisty, five foot nothing mayor to Floyd Bennett Field in Brooklyn. There, LaGuardia finally got off the plane and gave an impromptu press conference where he expressed the importance of an airport. They found a 105 acre spot just off the coast of Flushing Bay in Queens and made the marshy shores five times bigger with heavy duty landfill. There we built New York City Municipal Airport, LaGuardia Field, or simply "LaGuardia Airport".

HARLEM

The Harlem River, also an estuary, connects the East
River to the Hudson River just alongside the Community
known as Harlem, named after a Dutch town in the
Netherlands. This is largely an African-American
community up here, one of the largest in the country,
and a watershed for civil rights activity over the years.
Every major African American civil rights group has
had their headquarters up here in Harlem at one time or
another.

We tore down San Juan Hill to build Lincoln Center and
the Hispanics moved up here and found some affordable
housing next to the African-American neighborhoods as
the Italians who lived here followed the Irish into the

suburbs. The Spanish called this area "El Barrio" or what we call, Spanish Harlem. Some famous people from Spanish Harlem include writer Piri Thomas who wrote that book, _Down These Mean Streets_. This was required reading for many of us here in New York City public schools. Thomas had a history of running in these streets with gangs and crime. He ended up doing some time in prison where he turned his life around and wrote his book.

Another famous guy from Spanish Harlem was one of the original Mambo Kings, Tito Puente. From Puerto Rico, this decorated WWII Navy veteran who served in nine major battles, was discharged with a Presidential Commendation. Tito used the GI Bill to enroll in the famous Julliard School of Music, graduated and went on to win Six Grammy awards. Tito led the beat of Afro-Cuban and Caribbean music into mainstream America. Tito was popular through the clubs here in Spanish Harlem, like the world famous Cotton Club. It was the Puerto Ricans and Cubans from this neighborhood who were largely responsible for that movement. You might remember the early episodes of I Love Lucy where Ricky Ricardo was a Cuban musician. Until in the later episodes, after the Cuban Missile Crisis, the TV writers did all they could to make Ricky a Mexican!

HARLEM HELL FIGHTERS

Also from Harlem we got the Harlem Hell Fighters, the most decorated unit in all of World War I. The Hell fighters of the 369 Infantry Division fought in many of our country's wars but during WWI they made a noticeable impact for the Allies. Because of the segregation policy of the US Army, African-American soldiers could not fight alongside the white units. The U.S. government loaned them over to the French with specific orders to enforce segregation policies and by no means give them any weapons. So the Harlem Hell fighters had fought under the French flag. The French paid no attention to the American policy of segregation and gave the Hell fighters the weapons they needed to get the job done.

After three shipwrecks the Harlem Hell fighters were the first American unit to hit the ground in France and the first Allied unit to cross the Rhine River. When a unit of American Marines fired on the 369th, in true Hell Fighter spirit, they dug in and fired back. There were casualties on both sides.

Though the Hell Fighters took many casualties, they never backed up, never lost a foot of ground in the trench warfare, never had any one of them ever taken prisoner. They stayed in combat 191 days longer than any other American unit.

They won France's highest honor three times, the French Cross. Only recently did they get their Medal of Honor award, both as a unit and there was an individual soldier, Private Henry Johnson. This came from a joint effort between New York Governor George Pataki and Senator Hillary Clinton. Of the famous Harlem Hell fighters, you had celebrated band leader James Europe Reese, who brought their jazz music to Europe and the commanding officer of that World War I brigade was Colonel Benjamin O. Davis Sr. who went on to become the first African-American General in the United States Army.

THE BIG APPLE

A favorite question people ask me is why New York
City is called the big apple. The origin of this story is
unclear; there are a couple of good plausible tales that
can answer this. But the strongest and most believable
story I have ever heard is the one that comes from our
African-American jazz musicians that lived up here in
Harlem. They traveled from all over the country
working odd jobs as train porters and horse trainers
while playing music at night in clubs where ever they
ended up. Naturally, some cities paid more money to
hear jazz music than others. Sugar, was and still is, the
slang word for money. Sugar daddy, sugar momma or
sugar baby are all references to moneyed people.
Apples have the highest sugar content of any fruit
natively grown in North America. So these musicians

would travel around the country looking for who paid the most money to hear jazz music and nick-name these cities according to their sugar content. The city with the most gigs and best pay would be the big apple. They discovered that it was New York who paid the most money. We paid the most *sugar* to hear jazz. The term was revived after Frank Sinatra announced to the public on a live microphone that it was great to be back in the big apple. From that point on, many writers made parallels to the fact that most of the worlds gold bullion is stored below the Federal Reserve in downtown Manhattan. That Manhattan's average income is nearly three times that of the national average or that New York is the biggest income producing state in the union. But the Big Apple nickname is owed to the African American Jazz musicians of Harlem.

Harlem is also known for its churches. In fact there are more churches in Harlem than there are in any other city inside of New York City. Harlem has some famous parks too, like Kobe Park or Rutger, where they host the Rutger tournaments. This is where the kids who play street ball, get to play against the pros, who came down from the big leagues. The basketball scouts come down here and they look at the local talent. Years ago they found a kid here who came up on a bus from Philadelphia. He was a lanky seven foot one inch tall kid who had to borrow someone's sneakers to get on the court. They were several sizes too small but it didn't seem to thwart this kid's performance. He eventually made it to the pros and played for the Philadelphia franchise. To date he is still the only player to have scored 100 points in a single game all by himself. His name was Wilt Chamberlain and he did this in 1962 against, of all teams, our New York Knicks! Chamberlain played his first year in the pros on a team called, The Harlem Globetrotters who were not from Harlem, they were a team originally from Illinois. That was an elaborate marketing scheme by their creators.

Another kid they found on the basketball courts here came from uptown in Inwood, which was a couple of miles up the river. He actually played against Chamberlain in the Rutger Tournament while still in Power Memorial High School. He was a 7'2" tall only child named Lew Alcinder. He graduated from UCLA and was drafted by the Milwaukee Bucs but played a majority of his career for the Los Angeles Lakers. Somewhere along the way he had changed his name to Kareem Abdul-Jabbar. *"You are who you make people believe you are."* When Kareem retired from that Laker dynasty, he owned nine different basketball records and still is the leading scorer. He also has the record for most records, so that makes ten!

Kareem was a student of the kung-fu master and film star, Bruce Lee. He fought Lee in his final film *"Game of Death"* where Lee unexpectedly passed away before the filming was completed. Wilt Chamberlain fought action star turned governor, Arnold Schwarzenegger in one of the Conan movies. So the two kids from the Rutger Tournament both had their flirt with movie fame.

189

GOTHAM CITY

Gotham is another one of our cities nicknames. Gotham
is actually a city in the English town of
Nottinghamshire. It was a city out on the perimeter of
the kingdom where King John wanted to set up a base
camp in. However the bohemians of Gotham wanted
nothing to do with this so they rebelled. The king sent a
message saying he was going to come to Gotham and
since the people didn't want him to come through, they
started acting like morons. Perhaps figuring that if the
king could see how incompetent and silly Gotham was
he would lose interest in his idea of a post. So when the
king showed up, the citizens of Gotham acted like
complete imbeciles. It worked because the king went

through Gotham, just looked at all the insanity and abandoned his idea.

So due to the "foolish ingenuity" of Gotham's residents, the 17th century writer, Washington Irving, gave the name "Gotham" to New York City in his _Salmagundi Papers_ (1807). That's why New York is given the nickname Gotham City because people seem to do what they want here, whatever works.

RANDALL'S ISLAND

Randall's Island across the Harlem River is an island bound by the East River on its other side. Its park is where a famous Brazilian named simply, Pele used to play soccer. The lights on Randall's Island Park some of you might be old enough to remember that those are the lights that shinned on Ebbets Field when the Dodgers played in Brooklyn before moving to Los Angeles. They've since torn down Ebbets Field but saved those lights and put them over on Randall's Island. Those lights saw a 27 year old rookie come to the plate for the first time in 1947, and shatter the color barrier for African-Americans in major league baseball. His name was Jackie Robinson, his number was 42, and that number is retired in all of baseball.

Jackie Robinson spent ten years in the big leagues but afterwards became a champion in many civil rights movements. He got the first black bank open, The Freedom Bank, it's here in Harlem.

Those lights shine on the same track where Jessie Owens pre-qualified for the 1936 Olympic Games. This is something we still call to this day, the Nazi Olympics. Adolph Hitler was out to show the world racial superiority with his so-called master race of Aryan athletes were no match for the mongrel races of the world, like America. Many people don't know it but Jessie Owens qualified in only seventh place on the track over there. The kid who qualified in first place was a kid from Brooklyn, by the name of Marty Glickman. Glickman still has records that stand today at Syracuse University.

The head of the U.S. Olympic Committee in 1936 was the very controversial and open Nazi sympathizer, Avery Brundage. Brundage and track coach Dean Winters didn't want to upset Hitler, so they pulled Marty Glickman from the roster because they thought Glickman had too good of a chance to win and Glickman was Jewish. Instead, they put in the seventh place qualifying African-American who hurt his back on a staircase the night before the event. Jesse Owens being African American, wasn't permitted to dine with the whites on the team in the restaurant so the African Americans on the team had to eat in the basement.

Owens slipped on some grease and fell on the stairs, hurting his back. Well as most of you know, in the next 70 minutes Jesse Owens broke four world records! This incredible feat is widely considered to be one of the most amazing athletic achievements of all time. This would send Hitler storming out of the stadium, furious, humiliated and downright beaten.

Interestingly enough, Owens would later recount in his autobiography on how Hitler stood up and waved to him. He also quoted, *"I wasn't invited to shake hands with Hitler, but I wasn't invited to the White House to shake hands with the President, either."*

Now to Germany's credit, there was an athlete on the German team Lutz Long, who noticed that while Owens was pre- qualifying for the long jump, he fouled out in his first two attempts and a third foul would have eliminated Owens. So Lutz Long put a white towel just behind the foul line and asked Owens to jump off the towel. Jesse did and he won the gold in the long jump as well.

Over 110,000 people cheered Owens on in the stadium. Jesse Owens received celebrity status in the streets of Berlin where he spent hours signing autographs. Back home in the U.S.A. after he received a ticker-tape parade he attended a feast at the famous Waldorf-Astoria hotel but because of his color, Owens had to ride in the freight elevator to attend the feast in his honor.

In 1976 President Gerald Ford awarded Jesse Owens the Presidential Medal of Freedom. He was awarded the Congressional Gold Medal (posthumously) by President George H.W. Bush. A Street in Berlin was renamed for him and the Jesse Owens Realschule/Oberschule (a secondary school) is in Berlin-Lichtenberg.

After the games Owens had a hard time making a living so he became a sports promoter and an entertainer of sorts. He would give local sprinters a ten or twenty yard headstart and beat them in the 100 yard dash. He also challenged and defeated racehorses! Jesse Owens was a pack-a-day smoker for 35 years, he died of lung cancer at age 66 in Tucson, Arizona.

There were eighteen African-Americans in the 1936 Olympic Team and fourteen of them medaled. Another African American who medaled was Clifford Robinson, who was Jackie Robinson's younger brother. Robinson took the silver medal right on the heels of Jesse Owens in one of the races. So this is the Jackie Robinson – Jesse Owens coincidence of Randall's Island.

Marty Glickman went on to play professional basketball and professional football, one of the few athletes to do two pro sports in one career. Then he went on to become a celebrated sports announcer where he became the voice of the New York Giants and the voice of the New York Jets as well. He totally revamped the world of sports casting with his rapid-fire play-by-play of calling the game. He passed away in 2001 without ever getting apology from the U.S. Olympic Committee but not before publishing his autobiography, <u>The Fastest Kid on the Block</u>, the Marty Glickman story.

YANKEE STADIUM

The New York Yankees are either the greatest team ever or the best team money can buy. One thing is for sure, there's no middle ground with the New York Yankees; you either love them or you love to hate them. They play up in The Bronx in what is now the third oldest stadium in the league.

The New York Yankees started out as an expansion team from Baltimore called the New York Highlanders. They used to share the same stadium with the New York Giants when the Giants played in what we called the Polo Grounds here in Harlem. With the expansion of major league baseball, the Giants have long since moved

to moved to San Francisco. We tore down the Polo
Grounds and built the Polo Grounds projects in its place.

Being a new team the Highlanders were anxious to scout
some new players. They got themselves an ace pitcher
from the Boston franchise who had a no-hitter to his
credit and twenty-nine and a half scoreless innings in a
World Series game. Then he blew out his arm and
couldn't pitch any more. The owner of the Boston
franchise sold him to New York for a song; literally, a
song! He wanted to finance a Broadway play titled *"No,
No, Nanette"* (tea for two) and needed some quick cash.
The play went on a run and had mixed reviews, but not
as much as this player would have. New York put this
pitcher with the blown out arm in the outfield; who
knew he would go on to hit 714 home runs! His name
was George Herman (Babe) Ruth.

So many people came out to see Babe Ruth play
baseball that the Giants got jealous so they kicked the
Highlanders out of their stadium. The Highlanders
would cross the Harlem River, climb the cliffs of the
Bronx and take the Dutch word for Johnny - *"Yan-kee"*
and reinvented themselves. *"You are who you make
people believe you are."* And the New York Yankees
went on to become not only the greatest baseball team
ever but the most winning-est sports franchise in modern
history. They have Twenty-six world championships
and thirty-nine American League championships. The
Yankees are also the only team that is represented at
every position in the Baseball Hall of Fame and thirteen

players have their numbers retired on the outfield wall of Yankee Stadium. No other team in any other sport comes even close.

The dynasty of the Yankees started out with that legendary player, Babe Ruth. Babe is argued to be the greatest baseball player ever; he could pitch, he could hit, he could do it all. Babe hit a home run on the average every eleven and a half times at bat but he struck out a lot too. This drove his batting coaches crazy, they told him to forget about the long ball, he kept striking out too much. They told the Babe to stand at the plate and find that spot in the field that the players aren't standing in and focus on hitting the ball in that direction. Babe told them that they were not standing behind the outfield wall! "I swing big when I go up to the plate. I either hit big or I miss big but I never let the fear of striking out stop me from swinging big" and that's what he continued to do.

Over the years, many great Yankees would carry the torch for generations of fans. There was Lou Gehrig, they guy who they called the Iron Horse. Gehrig had set a record for 2130 consecutive games. There were also greats like Joe Dimaggio, Mickey Mantle, Roger Maris, Reggie Jackson, Thurmon Munson, Don Mattingly, and the Yankees of today like Derek Jeter and Bernie Williams.

Joe Louis knocked out Max Schmeling in Yankee Stadium and demystified another Nazi mystique. Other great heavy-weight battles would include Jack Dempsey, Rocky Marciano, Ingemar Johnson, Floyd Patterson, the Cinderella Man James Braddock and the greatest fighter of all time, Muhammad Ali. Elton John, The Rolling Stones, Led Zeppelin and Bette Midler all played concerts here. Two Popes celebrated Mass here and The Reverend Billy Graham sold it out! So it's not just baseball; its part of our culture and the New York Yankees played right here in the Bronx.

YOGI BERRA

My favorite Yankee though, was a guy that they called
Yogi Berra. Like Yogi, I was in the navy but unlike
Yogi, he was in during WWII. Yogi was on Omaha
Beach during the D-Day invasion fighting the Nazis.
Yogi, like some of the players of his day, took time out
of their professional career's to serve their country. Yogi
came home and won ten World Series rings. He has
more than anyone else in baseball; he's got one for each
finger!

However, Yogi is also famous for all those ridiculous
sayings that don't make any sense unless they're coming
from Yogi. He said things like ...

"Ninety percent of baseball is half mental."
"We made too many wrong mistakes."
"It gets late early out here."
"Nobody goes to that restaurant anymore -- it's too crowded."
"If you don't know where you're going, you might not get there."
"You better go to other people's funerals, or they won't come to yours."
"It's like deja-vu all over again."
"It ain't over till it's over."
"The future ain't what it used to be."

The list goes on, he's got dozens of them, they're called *"Yogi-isms"*.

THE BRONX

You might notice how when referring to the borough on the mainland, we New Yorkers put an article in front of it. We call this borough up here The Bronx, not Bronx. However we don't call it The Manhattan or The Queens. There's a reason for this and that is that The Bronx is the only borough named after a person, Jonas Bronck.

Jonas Bronck was a Swedish farmer, who sailed for the Danish Navy. He came over here in around 1641 to do some farming when the Dutch had the colony here called New Amsterdam. Bronck can quite possible be remembered as one of the most intrepid man in history. He wanted to come to America so bad, he actually taught himself how to captain boats, just so he could get here. However when he got into the Dutch Colony of New Amsterdam, he realized that Manhattan was mostly bedrock and where it wasn't bedrock it was swampy marshland and where it wasn't swampy marshland it was too wooded. There was no place to build a farm. So he did some soil samples in the surrounding areas and he found out that the area just across the river was perfect for what he wanted to do.

Bronck appealed to the Dutch governor to go over there to build a farm but the trouble was; the Dutch were at war with the Native Americans. The Dutch governor told Bronck that the Natives Americans don't have the same concept of real estate as we do in Europe. You see the Dutch didn't know that when the Native Americans accepted their gifts for this island that it meant that they had to leave. The Dutch didn't realize that Manhattan was the Native's prime hunting grounds and that many different Native tribes have been coming here for thousands of years to celebrate the bounty that he island offered. The Natives believed that the land, just like the sky and ocean was a gift from Mother Nature that couldn't be bought or sold but shared by all God's creatures. So the Natives paid no attention to the Dutch sovereignty and tried come on the island anyway. They hopped over the fences the Dutch built and picked fruits from the trees and hunted game in the Dutch backyards. This had caused a number of violent skirmishes between the two cultures. As a result the Natives where exiled off of Manhattan but camped out in places close by on the mainland.

The Dutch governor warned Bronck, the giant 6'9"
Swede that if he went over to the mainland that he'd be
on his own. That's just what he did; Jonas Bronck took
his three covered wagons over there. The Native
Americans surrounded him right away. He got up on his
wagon and he shouted to the natives that if they wanted
to kill him, they should do it now. This got their
attention. He said that what he had in his wagons were
the seeds of fruits and vegetables that they've never seen
before. Things that they needed over there in the colony
that they can't grow, they didn't have the soil. Bronck
managed to convince the natives that they had the soil
and he had the seeds so let's make a deal. He asked the
natives to give him five hundred acres so he could build
a farm; farm that he would teach them how to work
themselves. They would go into business together, and
if neither one of them were making any money after one
year, then he would just leave peacefully and they could
have it all.

The natives saw that the big Swede was different than
the Dutch and were curious to see what was in his
Trojan horse. They knew that when the white man came
here, that they were pretty much here to stay, they saw
more and more ships coming in every day. The Natives
also learned that the Anglo Europeans preferred a form
of currency called money. This was a new concept for
the Natives who had always relied on the barter system
up to now.

The natives gave Bronck the 500 acres asked for, and over the years they were making so much money that property kept doubling. Largely because Jonas Bronck didn't do something that everybody in Manhattan was doing. Manhattan was full of butcher shops, slaughter houses and here in Harlem was a fish market and they were happy to deliver it to people for an extra charge. Jonas Bronx didn't deliver. If you wanted your produce, you had to go to him; in other words, you had to go to "The Bronck's" farm to get it.

That's pretty good for a Swedish farmer. So the Romans say that those who endure conquer, Jonas Bronck got one of the five boroughs of the greatest city of all time named after him. The Broncks spelling was changed to Bronx when the British came and took the colony from the Dutch and it became a very popular vacation spot of the early New Yorkers. Nowadays we go out to the beaches of Long Island, called the Hamptons, or upstate to the Mountains called the Catskills but back then for quick weekend get-a-ways, vacationed in The Bronx. So that's why we call it "The Bronx".

HARLEM RIVER BRIDGES

High Bridge really isn't a bridge, it's an aqueduct. This is how we get our water. People in the nation's capitol in Washington D.C. drink the Chesapeake Bay. People in the great cities of Detroit and Chicago drink the Great Lakes. We here in New York City do NOT drink the Hudson or East Rivers. We get our water from the reservoirs upstate New York in the Catskills. This aqueduct links up to the Croton Reservoir. Some argue that it's the best drinking water in the country.

The tall tower in Manhattan next to High Bridge is a pump tower that facilitates water through this aqueduct. A very famous early American poet would come up here and get his inspiration to write, but sadly this guy would be dead long before he was famous. He was known as the father of gothic horror and the inventor of the American short story, his name was Edgar Allen Poe. This is where he sat to get inspired to write his chilling tales of death and macabre like The Raven, The Pit and the Pendulum, and the Tell Tale Heart.

There are two bridges in the Harlem River, that link up to major interstates on the east coast of America. The blue one is the Alexander Hamilton Bridge. It is named after the guy we mentioned earlier who was the first Secretary of the US Treasury. Of all of our founding fathers; Hamilton was the only immigrant, he was born in the British West Indies. The Alexander Hamilton Bridge hooks up to I-95 which runs up and down the east coast From Maine and ends up in (the sixth borough) Florida. The grey bridge just north of it, is the Washington Bridge named after George Washington, the father of our country. Washington actually has at least two bridges in the city named after him. The George Washington Bridge is on the other side of the island but the same street (178th) connects them.

We made George Washington our first president and put his portrait on the U.S. one dollar bill. The Washington Bridge here hooks up to U.S. Route number 1. So that's the hint; George Washington, first president, one dollar bill –Washington Bridge and George Washington Bridges go to Route US (number) 1.

Alexander Hamilton was a financial genius, I can't say it enough and he straightened out the books of the country.

This caused a lot of rancor and dissent amongst our founding fathers. Thomas Jefferson sent auditors after him on several occasions but Hamilton baffled even the most austere auditor. Hamilton had a secret; he never kept any of the money for himself. He considered his natural talent to be what he owed his country, his patriotic duty. He was well educated; thought he'd make his living as an attorney but he did so much pro-bono work that when was killed in that duel with Aaron Burr, he left his wife and seven children absolutely penniless. Our financial genius died broke.

Thomas Jefferson, the guy who had him audited wrote the Declaration of Independence and with his own hand he said that all men were created equal. Yet at the same time, he owned slaves. And George Washington who we say is the greatest military leader of all time, better than Alexander the Great, better than the Caesars and Charlemagne; had lost more battles than he won.

The point I'm making here is that our founding fathers were not perfect people; some could hardly stand each other and many mistakes were made along the way. But one thing that they all agreed on was that no one person should have so much power. They created a body of government that reflects a democracy. If anyone of them tried to stand alone, the system would collapse but we don't stand alone in this country, we are the United States of America. We have a system here, though far from perfect; it's the best system out there because it's set up of a system of checks and balances. So it doesn't matter if you sit a bit to the left or a bit to the right, if you're a Republican or Democrat, if you're House or if you're Senate, a Conservative or a Liberal, if you're elected or appointed because not one person gets too much power here. It's all set up in checks and balances, that's one of the reasons we are the only surviving superpower.

ROBERTO CLEMENTE

The first State Park in the city of New York is named
after a man from Puerto Rico, Robert Clemente.
Roberto Clemente wore number twenty-one in right
field for the Pittsburgh Pirates and that number is retired
there today. People will argue that Clemente was the
greatest right fielders to ever play the game. He had
three thousand hits at the plate, Twelve Golden Gloves
in the field, and a rifle of an arm. His ability to throw
perfect strikes to home plate from the warning track was
matched by only a few. But more than all the wonderful
things Clemente did on a baseball field, and there were
plenty, he is better remembered for his charitable acts of
humanitarianism off the field. He spent a good part of
his career giving thousands and thousands of his own

dollars to charitable causes. Sadly one such incident cost him his life. After an earthquake had ravaged the country of Nicaragua, Roberto Clemente sent down a plane full of money and relief aid for the victims. When he learned that the plane never got there he was upset. So on New Years Eve in 1972, Clemente packed up his own plane, with more money and relief aid and flew down to Nicaragua himself to help out who he could. Tragically his plane crashed and killed him in the prime of his life. But we'll remember him for the great humanitarian he was by naming the first State Park in the City of New York after him.

Remember that one-third of the people living here in New York City are of Hispanic descent. Robert Clemente is a personal hero of many people here in New York. Myself as well, we actually share the same birthday; August 18th. Roberto Clemente is the second baseball player to be put on a U.S. Postage stamp, the first one was Jackie Robinson.

Roberto Clemente and Jackie Robinson had a very similar saying, if you put the two together, it might sound something like this: *"Life is not a spectator sport; you can't spend it in the bleachers watching it go by. If you ever have the opportunity in life to make something right, you got to get up and take a stab at something, otherwise you're just wasting your time here."*

Major League Baseball gives the Roberto Clemente Award every year to the player who best follows

Clemente's example with humanitarian work. In 2002, Clemente was posthumously awarded the Presidential Medal of Freedom. In 2003, he was inducted into the U.S. Marine Corps Sports Hall of Fame. There is also currently a campaign underway to have all major league teams retire Clemente's number. Supporters cite an influence on baseball at least as strong as that of Jackie Robinson, whose number is also retired throughout MLB.

Sir COLIN POWELL

Born in The Bronx of immigrant parents from Jamaica we have Secretary Colin Powell. A kid who came from very humble origins, Powell was a product of New York City public schools both in the Bronx and in Harlem. He wasn't an exceptionally bright student but in college (CUNY) he joined the ROTC and found his calling. He then went in the army during the Viet Nam War and by the time *Desert Storm* came upon us; Powell was a four star general calling the shots. Under the Clinton Administration he was the Joint Chiefs of Staff, the highest ranking military officer. Then he served as the Secretary of the State under George W. Bush's Administration. He is now semi retired and is one of the Chairmen for Time-Warner and AOL. General Colin Powell is also one of the few people in the world to win the Presidential Medal of Freedom twice. He has also been knighted by the Order of Bath.

HECTOR CAFFERATTA Jr.

The Bronx has its share of war hero's too. We have a
Bronx born Puerto-Rican named Hector Cafferatta Jr.
At eighteen years old, Cafferatta side-stepped a very
promising career as a professional football player to
enlist in the Marine Corps and fight in the Korean War.
Private First Class Hector Cafferatta Jr. was the only
survivor of his entire Firing Team up that was wiped out
in a trench near the Chosan Reservoir. He called up on
the radio and asked for some back-up but the Marines
told him there was no back-up; his back-up was pinned
down on another hill. He'd have to do what he can on
his own, to secure that gap in the line himself.

So for the first time in four days, Pvt. Cafferatta took off his boots to warm his frostbitten feet over a fire and at that point the first wave of North Korean enemy charged his trench. Barefoot through the frozen snow, he slipped and slid his way manning four different machine gun mounts, firing upon wave after wave of charging North Korean enemy. They shot him down a couple of times but he kept getting back up and grabbing a different mount. He used the cover of night to give the impression to the Koreans that there were more people in the trench with him. They threw grenades in the trench at him. He picked up the live grenades with his bare hands and threw them back. One of them took off part of his hand, but he still kept going all through the night. When the morning finally came, they saw that he was the only man there and then all the rest of them charged him at once. Cafferatta fought them off with his shovel, bayonets and bare fists. No doubt fighting skills honed on the streets of the South Bronx. In the end, Pvt. Cafferatta was still was the last man standing. He won the nation's highest award, the Medal of Honor. World War I had Sergeant York and World War II had Audie Murphy, but the Korean War had our very own Hector Cafferatta Jr. from right here in the South Bronx. Now lives in New Jersey and he has a whole section of the highway named after him.

HIP-HOP

The Bronx was where Ragtime music got it roots. It has since evolved into the jazz culture. The Bronx is also the cradle of Hip-Hop. Hip Hop music (also referred to as Rap) is a style of popular music. It is made up of two main components: Rapping (MCing) and DJing (audio mixing and scratching). Along with breakdancing and graffiti (tagging), these compose the four elements of the whole Hip-Hop culture. A movement started by the inner-city youth (mostly minorities) in New York City in the mid 1960s.

The roots of hip hop music are deep in West African and African American music as well as poetry. Influences came from poets Jalal Mansur Nuriddin, Gil Scott-Heron and "The Greatest" fighter of all time; Muhammad Ali.

217

Ali was famous for rhyming his promotions. The kids idolized his brash style and were inspired to write their own rhymes. They would take the wax record discs and turn them in the opposite direction on the turntables back and forth in a style they called "scratching". Thus making their own music from somebody else's, then they inserted their own rhymes or "raps". Hence, rapping or rap music was born.

The MCs are the guys who introduce the DJs and keeps the audience excited. MCs began by speaking between songs, urging people to dance and entertaining the audience with jokes and anecdotes, keeping a "flow" to the events. Eventually this evolved into a more stylized form and became known as *rapping*.

Part of what started the whole Hip-Hop movement was a DJ and community leader from the South Bronx, named Afrikka Baambataa. During Bam's (his nickname) early years, he was a founding member of a street gang called the Black Spades (a gang that included boxing great, Iran Barkley). After a life-changing visit to Africa, he changed his name to **Afrika Bambaataa Aasim**. *"You are who you make people believe you are."*

Bam was influenced by the story of the Zulu Warriors in the film *"Zulu"*. Inspired, Bam used his leadership and natural organizing skills to turn those involved in the gang life into something more positive for the community. He founded *ZULU NATION*, a group that were made up of mostly racially and politically aware

Hip-Hoppers. Bam organized block parties all around the South Bronx and he was soon renowned as one of the best DJs in the business. In 1980, he produced *Soul Sonic Force's* landmark single, "Zulu Nation Throwdown".

Hip-Hop skyrocketted during the 1970s when block parties became common in New York City. The DJs at block parties began isolating the percussion breaks to hit songs, realizing that these were the most danceable and entertaining parts; this technique called *"break-beat"* was common in Jamaica and had spread via the substantial Jamaican community in New York City, especially the godfather of Hip-Hop, Kool DJ Herc.

Kool DJ Herc is a Jamaican-American musician and producer, generally credited as a pioneer of hip hop during the 1970s. He was the originator of *"break-beat deejaying"*. Herc is also well known for his massive high quality and high volume sound system, against which even superior DJs could not compete. Herc and his MC crew *"The Herculoids"* started a movement which the relationship between Hip-Hop and reggae became more important again with reggae artists and rappers collaborating with each other.

The commercialization of hip hop came with the release of two Hip Hop recordings: "King Tim III (Personality Jock)" by the Fatback Band, and "Rapper's Delight" by The Sugarhill Gang. "Rapper's Delight" became the first Top 40 hit on the U.S. Billboard Pop singles chart.

Break-dancing was another art form where the kids
in the neighborhood created a dance of seemingly
gravity defying moves like the "moonwalk" or the
"head-spin." Some of their moves made their bodies
look boneless; a dance style they called "popping". A
series of acrobatic moves that were dares to each other
to see who could be outdone.

Graffiti was an interesting art and the only crime of
Hip-Hop. It's a form of vandalism, defacing public
property, not to mention any copyright infringements.
Graffiti writers as they prefer to be called (not artists)
would take their names; of course not their real names
(graffiti is a crime) they would take their street names
and then take the street that they lived on, which was
usually a number. They pushed the two together to form
an identification piece, a logo, or a "tag" as they called
it. They would paint them in the psychedelic colors of
the sixties and seventies and stretch the letters and
numbers out into their own handwriting called *"Wild
style"*.

*"In the beginning there was the word and the word was
a name and the name of the game was to get your name
up there in as many places as you could, for as long as
you could."* The quest to become famous but remain
anonymous was the graffiti writer's conundrum. These
writers would hang their pieces or tags on as many
buildings, schoolyards, handball courts that they could

find but there was nothing that the graffiti writers liked better than trains.

The train yards in New York City were a watershed for graffiti writing. Trains uptown and in the outer boroughs do something very different than the lines in downtown do. The trains up here, in most parts, run above ground. They get to leave this part of town and parade around the rest of the city like floating billboards advertising these kids artwork. That was part of the game, getting their names "seen".

Now in all fairness to the city, it is known that about 95% of the graffiti was crap. It was filthy, dirty, vulgar, sexist, racist and didn't belong on the trains. However the real artists knew that the city would cover up the dirty graffiti first, their whole mission was to keep their names up there as long as they could. The city would enter a multi-million dollar, multi-decade battle against the graffiti bandits but the graffiti writers were the largest, all volunteer, multi-ethnical organization in the city.

The city made it illegal to sell paint and markers to minors, which didn't do anything because the true graffiti artists didn't consider it *"real"* graffiti unless the paint and markers were stolen! Not that it meant the paint was stolen from stores so much as stealing it from each other. If you wanted to be a true graffiti "King" and known city wide, you couldn't just paint your own neighborhood trains, everyone in your neighborhood

knew who you were. You had to go into other train
yards in other parts of the city and tag (paint your name)
on those trains. This might mean you had to fight those
gangs in those areas and the losers of the fights would
have to give up their paint. If you're going to paint
trains with other people's paint in their yards, you get
that kind of fame. All at the same time, you had to
defend your own trains. This led to a series of other
crimes, up to and including murder. More than a few
times have track workers come to work in the morning
to find kids murdered, still clutching spray paint cans.

The city tried many different ways to thwart the graffiti
on the trains. They tried fences with razor wire but the
kids just clipped their way through it. They even had
wolves put in the train yards to scare the kids but wolves
don't attack men. The city gave paint remover loaded
with Agent Orange to the track workers to scrub off the
paint, something the graffiti writers called *"the orange
buff"* but as fast as they buffed the paint off, it was right
back on very often in the same day. The track workers
complained that the solution was making them sick so
they stopped using it after a while.

Then the city switched their train of thought, since they
couldn't take the paint away, what they did was coat all
the trains in a high polyurethane glossy coat of paint
where no paint would stick, it would simply wipe right
off. They used scratch resistant glass for the windows
and marker proof seats. Now the trains in New York
City's subway system are 99% graffiti free. Graffiti was

then forced back into the underground but not before quite a few made a name for themselves.

Just when the graffiti began to disappear, tattoo parlors in New York City that had been illegal for many years became legal again. Some writers opened up tattoo parlors. People from all over the world come to the Bronx to get tattooed by some of the famous graffiti writers. Some writers got a little more technical and build web-pages and design CD covers for musicians.

BROADWAY

Broadway is not only the oldest street in America, it's also the longest. It starts in lower Manhattan at One Broadway; that is the oldest address in America. One Broadway is where the Dutch landed and made the deal with the natives for that piece of property. Broadway runs all the way up to Albany, out State capitol.

Broadway is synonymous with live entertainment here in New York City. When people come to New York their entertainment for the most part is live, not like that fake Hollywood movie crap. Live performers all over the world hold their theatrical credits to those of the standards of Broadway, New York City, or Off-Broadway or even Off-Off-Broadway. This has nothing to do with the Street in Manhattan though; this is according to the seat count in the theater. A Broadway Production is any theater that has 500 or more seats and appeals to the mass audience. It doesn't matter what street the theater is on. Along with London's West End theatre, Broadway theatre is considered the highest level of English language theatre. Currently there are thirty-nine "Broadway" theaters in Manhattan. An Off-Broadway theater is a theater that has between 100 and 499 seats and an Off-Off-Broadway production is any theater that had 99 seats or less. These theaters are what we also call "black-box theater."

COLUMBIA UNIVERSITY

Bordering the Harlem Shipping Canal, through the trees, is Columbia University's Athletic Complex. Columbia University is an *Ivy League* (IV) school here in New York City the highest level you can go, as far as colleges go. Columbia University used to be called King's College when the British had the colony but now that we won our independence from Great Britain; we have no more allegiance to a king. So we changed the name to Columbia. *"You are who you make people believe you are."*

Among the earliest students and trustees of King's College were John Jay, the first Chief Justice of the United States; Alexander Hamilton, the first Secretary of the Treasury; Gouverneur Morris, the author of the final draft of the United States Constitution; and Robert R. Livingston, a member of the five-man committee that drafted the Declaration of Independence.

Of the first class to graduate Columbia College was a protégé of Alexander Hamilton who stood head and shoulders above everyone around him. His name was DeWitt Clinton also known by his nickname "Magnus Apollo". He was a former Senator of New York, a three time mayor of our city, a two time governor of our state, a state legislator and former presidential candidate. He will be forever known as the mastermind behind one of the eight wonders of the world, The Erie Canal. With that he did more for New York politically than any other politico up to or since.

Columbia's notable alumni now include: Three current United States Senators, sixteen current Chief Executives of Fortune 500 companies, and thirty-seven Nobel Prize winners have degrees from Columbia. Three of the eleven richest Americans have a degree from Columbia. Both president Roosevelts passed through Columbia Law school.

Other notable Columbia's alumni include: Rodgers and Hammerstein, Herman Wouk, Jack Kerouac, Allen Ginsberg, Art Garfunkel, Robert Moses, John Jacob Astor III, Warren Buffet, Isaac Asimov, Langston Hughs, James Renwick Jr., Upton Sinclair, James Cagney, Terrence McNally, John Stevens, Lou Gehrig and Sandy Koufax.

SPLIT ROCK

Across the canal from Columbia's athletic complex, you can see a very tall rock, about seventy feet high, and you will see the big blue with white trim "C" on it. That "C" stands for Columbia, that's the rowing teams' freshman tradition. They have to come out and touch it up every year.

This rock is called Split Rock, the story was loosely featured the movie "Basketball Diaries" with Leonardo DiCaprio. The legend of Split Rock goes that if your father or grandfather jumped off this rock; then you have to jump off it as well. They tell us in psychology classes that *"the child must die before the man can be born."*

Women pass into adulthood naturally, they bring life into the world but men need to go into manhood socially. Since the beginning of time, our elders have set us apart from boyhood by many daring tasks. Some tribal regions in the world today put their young boys in the ice or the forest or the jungle for a couple of days where they have to survive on their own. In many cases the young men have to slay a ferocious beast or accomplish some other heroic feat to be accepted into the fraternity of *"men"*. Here in the Bronx, you jump off a rock! The highest point on top is called Big Jazz and lowest point is Chicken's Leap. The level you choose to jump off, that's your link in the food chain!

The kids here like to do this in the summer months when the water is warmer. They love to do it when the Circleline boats come by because first of all they get an international audience. Secondly, it is a long standing Circleline tradition for the passengers to throw dollar bills into the water for the kids to leap off and grab after their feat.

THE PALISADES

Straight across the Hudson River from the Spyten Dyvel
Bridge, we have the New Jersey Palisades. This was
purchased for a hundred thousand dollars in 1903. The
Catholic Church, the Rockefellers and the State of New
Jersey own it. They all have an agreement that they will
not build on it. The Palisades must be preserved like
this until the end of time. The same thing goes for the
last 118 acres of Manhattan, Inwood Park.

Just like Central Park; this 118 acres of park like
preserve called Inwood Park can't be touched. This gift
from the Rockefellers, according to the treaty we have
with them, is the promise that we can't build on it. This
park is the, *what and the why* the Native Americans

called it, Manna-hatta; Island of Plenty (or prosperity). As this entire island was teaming with wildlife, for this is what all of Manhattan used to look like from the beginning of time, like one big clump of broccoli floating in the river. The only thing you will see disturbing this pristine view is a castle, just above the tree line. This is yet another gift from the Rockefellers, the Cloisters museum.

THE CLOISTERS

John D. Rockefeller Jr., like many of us had a
fascination with the Middle Ages. He went over to
Europe and found eleven abandoned monasteries, nearly
a thousand years old at various stages of decay. He
bought them from the European governments and hired
master stone masons to go over there and take them
apart brick by brick. Carefully they numbered each
brick and rock and in specific detail. Then they put
them on barges and shipped them over here where we
had a multi-million dollar consortium of artists,
architects and historians reconstruct of the eleven half or
so monasteries, they were able to complete four castles
as close as they could to the actual specifications.
Rockefeller had them filled with a vast array of art and

culture from the Middle Ages. But that's not where it ends, that's only where it begins.

The Rockefellers wanted you to go into their museum and not only see the famous Flemish Unicorn tapestries but they wanted you to look out the windows and see the same thing that they saw a thousand years ago. From the rear windows of the cloisters museum are the sights you saw when you look out those windows almost 1000 years ago. It's nothing but pristine wilderness; trees, mountains, rocks and the river. This is something only a Rockefeller could do; go back a thousand years and buy a piece of time, cross an ocean, land on another continent and set it up here in the largest of urban jungle in the United States of America.

This all contributes to that "love/hate" relationship we have with the rich here, in our city. Famous Beatle John Lennon used to say, "*If all the birds in the forest sung the same song, it wouldn't be what you call music*".

The Rockefellers made their fortunes as robber barons in Standard Oil, amongst other conglomerates, of the nineteenth, twentieth, and twenty-first Centuries. They were the world's first billionaires, they take that number one spot on the list of the richest people of all time but they did give a lot back too. The Rockefellers gave us many museums like this and churches, a lot of hospitals with forward thinking doctors making advances in human science and medicine and they gave us a lot of colleges too. Academies, so that average people like many of us can at least have the opportunity to pass through their institutions of higher learning to find out what it is we do best. Perhaps discover our genius and get a chance to hopefully to put something in the world with our name on it, something that will perhaps outlive us a long time after we check out.

So that personifies the bittersweet relationship we have with the rich and the super rich in the city. They're here and they're as different or diverse as anyone else as part of the many different cultures colliding and co-existing here in the urban forest of New York City.

I always say; that it is New Yorkers who put the city in diversity"

THE ERIE CANAL

If you go about 150 miles north of the George Washington Bridge, you'll get to our capital; Albany. That's where this river takes an interesting turn, you go left and you're in the Erie Canal.

The Erie Canal is a man-made ditch, a canal dug out clear across the State of New York. It goes some 365 miles long and connects the cities of Albany to Buffalo; it connects The Hudson River to the Great Lakes and thus connecting New York City to the Mississippi River, hence the middle of America. We built that canal in 1825 when the longest canal of the day was just twenty miles and most were just under two. With the completion of the Erie Canal, we passed up every other city in shipping, thanks to our then Governor DeWitt Clinton. Because of the Erie Canal, cities like Chicago, Detroit, Cleveland, Pittsburg and Cincinnati all became very wealthy cities because they all got to partake in trade along the route of the Erie Canal.

THE
GEORGE WASHINGTON
BRIDGE

The George Washington Bridge is the longest
suspension bridge in the world when it went up in 1930.
It's now only the fourth longest in the country but it is
the busiest. It's got fourteen lanes of traffic on two decks
moving very slowly twenty-one hours a day!

The steel cables on the Brooklyn Bridge will connect us
to London, the steel cables in the George Washington
Bridge, will go around the equator four and a half times.
The GWB is a Revolutionary War monument named
after George Washington, the father of our country and
his right hand man, General *"Light horse"* Harry Lee.
This Bridge connects the too cities of Washington

Heights Manhattan to Fort Lee New Jersey after the two great generals of the Revolutionary War.

Those of you not familiar with *Light horse* Harry Lee, are probably more familiar with his son. Lee's son graduated West Point Military Academy fifty miles up the river, at top of his class and went on to become the General of the Confederate Army of the Civil War, his name was Robert E. Lee.

ULYSSES S. GRANT

Lee's nemesis graduated at the very bottom of his class at and was arguably the worst cadet that ever went through West Point Military Academy. He went on to become the General of the Union Army in the Civil War, then the eighteenth president of the United States of America and now the portrait on the U.S. Fifty Dollar bill. His name was Ulysses S. Grant, though he wasn't born Ulysses, he was born Hiram Grant and he wasn't born here in New York City but he did spent the last part of his life with us. He was born in Ohio, where he grew up with Attention Deficit Disorder (ADD) and dyslexia.

Grant was a troubled and mischievous young man and anybody that knew him in his youth gave him the same nickname, *"Useless."* He graduated high school barely, his grades weren't good enough to get him into any college. Grant's parents didn't know what was troubling him all the time and couldn't figure out why he couldn't read so well. They thought he was just plain lazy but they didn't think it wasn't anything that the army couldn't straighten out.

Grant's mother went to High School with who turned out to be their congressman so she called on him for a favor. Their congressman obliged as he had some connections at West Point. He filled out Grant's application himself and sent it in. He put the initials U.S. in the top corner where Grant's first name should've been. This was his code to his cronies on the panel that this kid isn't smart enough to be here. This was personal favor so when he shows up, make him work.

Grant showed up to the academy and sees the application. He noticed the letters in the corner and rather than bring attention to the fact he's there on a favor, he changes his name to start with the letters U and S. There aren't many to choose from but here's where Grant's curse of dyslexia became a blessing; *Useless became Ulysses! "You are who you make people believe you are."*

Though Grant finished at the bottom of his class, he discovered his natural genius. Grant turned out to be a brilliant military strategist. His talents even to this day are rarely matched. George Washington is said by most historians to be the greatest military leader of all time but Grant is said to be the most enigmatic.

Grant took a commission as a Lieutenant and fought a stint in the Mexican War, a war Grant was outwardly spoken against. He felt we had no business taking land from Mexicans. He drank heavily at times and mouthed off to his superiors quite a bit. As a result, Grant always found himself assigned to the worst situations but his strategies always prevailed. Grant was always victorious, so much so that he got promoted to Captain. When the war ended, Grant continued drinking and mouthing off and then got himself kicked out of the army on insubordination charges.

Grant returned home disgraced with a Dishonorable Discharge and took a menial job as a clerk in his father's store. This wasn't a very colorful job for a war hero so Grant's boredom led to depression and some more drinking.

When the Civil War broke out, it wasn't long before the army realized that maybe they may have acted a bit too prematurely in their dismissal of Grant. He was a West Point graduate, combat experienced but most of all, they remembered Grant best for his strategy on the battlefield. So the army called him back in and sent him to war. Grant, though his strategies cost him a lot of lives, was always victorious. His victories got him promoted to General and eventually General of the

Union Army. This cause a lot of jealousy amongst some of the other Union Generals, they had cornered President Lincoln in his office one day and complained to him about Grant. They told President Lincoln that Grant was getting too many guys killed and that he drank too much. Lincoln scolded those Generals and told them to find out whatever Grant was drinking and to get a case of it for themselves! Lincoln reminded the Generals that Grant fights and wins and that was all he was interested in.

Grant's victories ended the Civil War. When the Civil War ended he was the most popular man on the planet. He became the eighteenth president of the United States of America largely on his popularity but from there, things would start to go bad for him.

Ulysses S. Grant became the 18th President of the United States and in all fairness to the presidency; Grant wasn't really one of the better ones we had. He did serve two terms as the commander in chief but had a lot of problems within his cabinet. Grant appointed his cabinet positions to his war buddies and people he owed favors to for getting him in the White House. This made his cabinet rife with incompetence at best and corruption at worst.

Presidents that succeeded Grant would learn two valuable lessons from his tutelage as the President. One, a political genius and a military genius are two different animals altogether. Grant, probably not knowing any

better, tried to run his presidency like he ran his army.
A brilliant military leader doesn't necessarily mean
you're going to be a good political leader. And two, find
competent people you can trust to staff your cabinet
with.

Grant tried to run for a third term, but the country was so
out-of-whack by then that his own party, (Republican)
turned their backs on him, they sent him up the road
with a handshake. That's a nicer way of saying that
Grant was financially, on his own.

Grant spent the next few years traveling around the
world with his wife, Julia. They were always well
received in countries as far away as Japan and Russia.
But then his sons got themselves thrown in jail. Using
Grant's last name they opened a savings and loan
institute with a greedy silent partner that swindled
people out of their entire life savings. Their firm went
"belly-up", the silent partner disappeared and Grant's
sons went to jail.

Grant always took responsibility for his men; on the
battlefield, in his cabinet and most certainly his sons. So
he stepped up to the plate, spent the last of his money
and even hocked his highly valuable civil war equipment
to pay for his sons crimes. Just around that time Grant
came down with a very painful cancer of the throat and
he learned it was terminal. So broke, sick and dying,
Grant was scrounging around for ways to make some
money before he checked out to leave behind for his

family. When you're as popular as Grant was; you make
a few friends. Of them was the award winning publisher
Joseph Pulitzer. Pulitzer found it interesting if we had a
president live here in New York City, we hadn't had one
up to this point; this was still before the Roosevelts. So
Pulitzer sent one of his writers out to find Grant and
make him an offer he couldn't refuse.

This writer found President Grant, not a hard thing to do,
Grant was still very popular and he always had a huge
following. This writer pulled Grant aside and must have
said something like: "Mr. President, we realize you had
some financial troubles and maybe we can help out.
New York City never had a president live here before;
we'd like you to be the first. Why don't you come out
there and live with us? We'll pay for the move, in fact
we'll set you up in any house that you want and the
exchange is; well let's face it Mr. President, you lived a
very interesting life, we'd like to make a book out of it.
Sell us your life story, we will publish your memoirs and
split the profits 50/50, we think it will do quite well."

Here, Grant would get yet another opportunity in life to
reinvent himself again. He'd become Grant the writer
and come out here to New York City with his wife Julia.
He spent the last part of his life writing his memoirs and
although he was crippled with this very painful cancer,
he was determined to get this book done before he
checked out. When he finally finished it, the writer read
it over and shook his head in disbelief. In fact he swore
to his publisher that he'd never changed one word, and

furthermore he said, "I only wish I could have written a novel this well". This writer's name was Samuel Langhorn Clemens but most of you probably know him by his pen name, Mark Twain.

The book was published but just days before it hit the stands; Grant lost his final battle with cancer. But like the brilliant military strategist lived his life and fought his wars, he died in the battle that won the war. Grant's death generated the publicity that this book needed to sell and sell big it did. Nearly a million dollars in proceeds and the writer and publisher true to their word would split this fifty/fifty with his wife, Julia. Julia would come into a windfall of nearly a half a million dollars and this was more than enough money she needed to spend out the rest of her life in financial comfort. When she passed away in 1902, they entombed her alongside of her husband in what happens to be the second largest mausoleum in the Western Hemisphere. This was all paid for by private money, no government funds went into this mausoleum. Grant had a huge following of friends and fans that all chipped in and gave him a great big "send-off".

Pretty good for a kid with dyslexia and attention deficit disorder. How would you have liked to be President at your 20th annual high school reunion? I'll bet he had a mouthful for all those kids that called him useless!

THE GREAT FIRE OF 1835

Other things you'll see in New York that people point
out are the tanks on top of the buildings. If you guessed
that they are water towers then you are correct. They're
up there because of a law; not just a civil law, but a law
of gravity that the Romans knew long before we did.
The Romans realized that water loses its pressure after
five stories; that is why there were no livable Roman
structures taller than. But Rome was an empire that had
the ability to expand outwards. We can't do that we're
an island. Again, we can't go out, we have to go up.
After the Revolutionary War, when New York City
became the place to be, people came here by the
millions and buildings started to go up in places you'd
never thought you'd see buildings. Like on top of
buildings, People start to live in structures six, seven,
even as high as nine stories tall without any water

pressure. They didn't care; they would rather deal with the inconvenience of no water pressure than to not live on the island.

Then one day in 1835 the unthinkable happened, the second most tragic fire that happened in America happened right here in New York City. Second only to the great Chicago fire; a fire burned here for four of the coldest days in December. A fire that destroyed twenty square blocks of Wall Street area and did in excess of $40,000,000 worth of damage. The great fire of 1835 took over 1,900 firemen from several hundred miles around to come and try and put out this fire. In the end, this fire put twenty-seven of the twenty-nine fire insurance companies out of business and that's when we realized we needed new rules. Many of them obsolete due to the advances of technology but one that remains is; any buildings over five stories high must have a water tank with one third of the water preserved for fire fighting purposes. That's why they're up there; the original ones are built out of cedar wood. Cedar wood is waterproof and could virtually last forever.

If you don't see a building with a water tower on top of it, it's on the inside. We started to do this after World War II. Our architects started to get a little bit more cosmopolitan about the way our city was looking so the newer buildings would hide the water towers. On the older buildings you could still see them. If you live in a five-floor walk-up like me, you don't need a water tower, but six floors and up gets them.

WRAP-UP

The elevated section of the highway on the west side of Manhattan is named after Joe DiMaggio, one of the all time great players of The New York Yankees. Now, as I mentioned in an earlier chapter, Yogi Berra is my favorite Yankee. We were both in the navy and we both say stupid things that people laugh at. However, Joe DiMaggio said something that I keep kind of close and I want to share it with you. Now first, Joe DiMaggio was the kind of player that went out every play of every game and played his absolute best. He never looked for the easy way out or had a lazy day in his whole career. When a sports writer asked him why he played so hard all the time, DiMaggio must have thought this was the dumbest question he ever heard. But he gave him an honest answer. He said *"That's because every time I go out there, there's always somebody watching me for the first or last time, I owe them my best."*

New York is city where a man, 76 years old, named John Stevens invented a train. That train took us off into a new age, The Industrial Age. It goes to show you, that it's never too late to find out your natural talent or too young either. Cornelius Vanderbilt at just fifteen years old made his mark in the ferries and saw a future in trains. He took three defunct railroads and merged them together into one. Everyone told him he'd loose his fortune and be ruined. But he followed his intuition and he became the most powerful railroad magnate the world had ever seen and the third richest person of all time.

They told George Washington that he'd never get this rag tag bunch of militiamen to overthrow the most powerful government of its time. Well, here we are a free and independent nation. Even George Washington turned around and told Thomas Jefferson that a nation of all men that are created equal would never last. Here we are now, the only surviving superpower. Even Thomas Jefferson turned around and told Governor DeWitt Clinton not to dig the Erie Canal. Two engineers already went bankrupt and out of business. Jefferson thought Clinton would go broke and bankrupt the State and possibly the entire union.

Now Governor Clinton knew that Thomas Jefferson bought the Louisiana Purchase from Napoleon, Clinton knew that Jefferson, a southerner, was going to try and hatch a plan that would take the capitol of America from New York City and move it down to the Gulf of Mexico region. Jefferson wanted to move the capitol to access the Mississippi River directly; that was where he saw the future of shipping. Governor Clinton knew he had to do something to keep the capitol here in New York City were all the banks and Wall Street was. Clinton knew that he had to somehow get to the Mississippi River. So Clinton put a tax on ordinary table salt and he dug that 365 mile ditch clear across the state of New York. That is where, when and how New York City passed up every other city in shipping. The rest of the cities on the east coast still had to spend a hundred dollars a ton on horseback or oxen to cross the rugged Appalachian Mountains.

But after the Erie Canal opened in New York; it only cost about six dollars per ton to go on barges that steamed through the canal system. A canal that paid for itself inside of a week of opening, thanks to the brainchild of Governor DeWitt Clinton, The Erie Canal. His canal was called *Clinton's ditch* in a mocking way by those who opposed it before it was completed and then by those who favored it when it was completed as a mockery to those very nay-sayers.

They told John Roebling that his steel cables would never hold up the Brooklyn Bridge; that the first gust of wind over forty miles an hour will knock it over. The Brooklyn Bridge is over 120 years old and counting and with proper maintenance it will last another 120 years, no problem. They told Clifford Holland that his ventilation system would never clean the air out of the tunnels; this tunnel is almost two miles long! Well the tunnels they dig today dozens of times longer, still use Clifford Holland's schematic for the ventilation system. It's kind of hard to improve on a 90-second turn around.

These people we mentioned here in this book were just a handful of many people who have been coming here for thousands of years; from the world over. They listened to their muse, found their genius and followed their souls. They had the discipline and the right attitude to make their own luck. That is the fundamental difference between those who make it and those who don't.

New York is a city that's driven by character. Characters who contributed something or some part of themselves to us. New York City, itself is a character; with a personality of its own and all who are here, feel it almost immediately. The city gives off a vibe of its own; a pulse that you feel from the moment you first set foot on any of its streets.

So there you have it; from the natives, the explorers, the settlers and to our founding fathers. The engineers and the inventors; the entertainers and the athletes; the politicians and the war heroes and the many other people that we didn't get to mention. *"You are who you make people believe you are."* Listen to your muse and follow your soul and perhaps you too will find your natural genius. YOU and only you can make that happen and I hope that these stories I gave you, will inspire you to do just that. Now give this book to someone you like then get out there in our city and do it.

WHAT TO DO

Take advantage of as many of the things here that we talked about in this book. Take a ride out to Ellis Island and look up that relative of yours that might have come through there, you may be surprised with emotion when you see their name on the wall there. While you are there you'll want to go see the lady, take a ride out to the Statue of Liberty as well. Go to the top of the Empire State Building and see what it's like to be on top of the world; seeing what King Kong saw. See a show on Broadway, you can get your tickets half price for shows that night at the TKTS booth on 47th Street and strangely enough, Broadway. Go to the museums on either side of Central Park, like the Museum of Natural History. There is a great big blue whale hanging from the ceiling, do not leave home without seeing that. They have a wonderful collection of dinosaur bones and other exhibits as well. Next door is the Rose Science Center or Hayden Planetarium where you get to see the stars.

Go beyond the boroughs, take a walk across the Brooklyn Bridge, everybody should do that at least once in their life, it's free. Get up to the Bronx to see the Yankees play baseball, also see the Bronx Zoo. It's the world's famous zoo where we put you people in cages and let the animals run free. You might like that experience. If you're broke, don't waste time in your hotel room yelling at the television set;

take a bed sheet out to the great lawn in Central Park and just watch people all day; you'll have the time of your life.

We hope that you continue on in your patriotic fervor while you're here in the city and take advantage of our ethnic diversity by eating in a family owned business you find in these neighborhoods like Chinatown and Little Italy. In fact one of our favorite delis is right on the corner of 43rd Street and 11th Avenue called *"ACE GOURMET SHOPPE."* A family from Trinidad owns it and they dole out generous portions of fresh food for your money.

You can get a real flavor of the city on Ninth Avenue. Ninth Avenue has the most eclectic collection of restaurants you'll find anywhere in the world. Everything from Afghani to Zimbabwean food is over there, somewhere on Ninth Avenue. One of our favorite places is Amarone on 47th Street and Ninth Avenue. The family is right off the boat from Italy and everything in the kitchen is made from scratch. They have a sidewalk café and a nice mixture of locals, celebrities and tourists as their clientele. Another great place is just up the block on 52nd Street you got Xing, arguably the best Chinese restaurant in the city outside of Chinatown. Try some sushi, the raw fish you see in all the New York movies and TV shows, sushi bars are over there, everywhere on Ninth Ave. You might want to try something different: How about Afghani food? At 52nd Street and Ninth Avenue is a place called Afghani Kabob. *Remember, we are at war "in" Afghanistan, not "with" Afghanistan;* big difference and their food is delicious! If that is too exotic for you then we have the all American diners like the Renaissance Diner where you can get the burger, shake and fries just as well. Just walk up or down Ninth Avenue and you'll see their menus posted in the windows. They display what they serve and the price and they'll be glad to have you. You'll see some celebrities up there that's where they live and that's where they hang out.

Stay away from the franchises, save those for the highway stops on the roadside. The money spent in a family owned business goes into our community and then back to yours. That's how the economy works best, when we keep the money going around. The money you spend in a franchise usually just goes into a bank in the Cayman Islands and chances are that's where it ends and what good is that?

But it is up to you, it's your money and you spend it however way you like. We're just glad you're spending it here. Your money will either come back to you or it won't but there is one thing I must caution you on how to spend here; there is one thing that you do have to watch closely and that is your "TIME". We really don't know how much time we have left here, do we? On September 11, 2001; 3000 people went to work one day, and they had their time taken from them in the most obscene way. If we learned anything from all that, we learned to start making the most of our time by making every minute we can, count.

15,000 years ago The Hudson River was just white water rapids, rushing out to the Atlantic Ocean. Fifteen thousand years from today it will be back to the white water rapids. You see we are all born in a very special time, so let's not waste it. We all have that special gift inside of us, so let's go find out what it is. It's up to us to make our move. How will they remember our names? That's a question we're going to have to answer after we close our eyes for the last time.

Keep in touch with me folks; let me know how you did. I have a nice collection of Emails and pictures from people all over the world that took my tour and I want you to add to it. My next book is going to be about you. I am taking the best New York stories from the passengers who took my cruise and I am going to put them together in this book. So please send them in.

newyorktalk@aol.com

Thank you.

ACKNOWLEDGEMENTS

As hard as we try, most of us can not write a book on our own. Although it is our name that appears on the cover, it takes a team of dedicated professionals who share your dream that we need to consistently rely upon for support and inspiration.

My biggest source of inspiration came from my audience; the passengers, who came from all over the world to my shows and have left our ships motivated to go out and make the most of their time in the city. I have received from them dozens of email letters every season thanking me for a wonderful tour but I cannot thank them enough for their stories.

I thank my peers, the other tour guides and crew members of the Circleline who have taught me a lot about the city. These guides include Tim Hollon, John and his son Chris Mason, Jim Horn, John Keats, Tom Wurl, John Curran, Dave Parker, Bill Brown and the immortal Steven Moran. Captains; Ed Weber, Joe Tierney, Mike "Mad Dog" Duffy, Brian Brennan, Alan Michael, Jimmy Olsen, Keith Possaint, Kenny Cochran, Richie "Sugar" Naruszewicz, Greg Hanchrow, Vito Gualtieri and Eric Johansen also contributed greatly their vast knowledge and experience to this work. Their crews also provided clear examples of leadership, professionalism and selfless knowledge to their passengers as well as this work.

This undertaking would've never gotten of the ground if it weren't for the professionalism of Chris Calhoun and his dedicated staff at Circleline Sightseeing Cruises. From the line catchers and all the way up to the presidents Robert Maher and Andreas Sappok, they unselfishly sacrificed much of their rare "free time" during the hectic summer season to answer my endless questions.

Captain Mike Keena; who sponsored me into United Marine Division, Local 333. The union largely responsible for the revitalization of the nearly forgotten, majestic waterfront of New York City. GO UNION!

Of course we cannot leave out our favorite restaurant, if not for the staff of Amarone, we wouldn't have a place to send anyone to enjoy the perfect New York experience. Their food is hot, the drinks are cold and I don't know the names of the songs they play. They fit right in with the character of New York City in Hell's Kitchen. Their international staff are always happy to serve food made from scratch "in the old world" style from their kitchen. The crowd there is also a reflection of the diversity our city has to offer. Everyone from locals, tourists, politicians and celebrities dine along side of each other to round out their New York experience.

I would also like to thank: writers; Tom Kelly, TJ English, Jack Ketchum, Dan Rode, Mike Indemaio, Raul Correa, Jimmy Schwatzman, Anthony Bourdain and especially Maryanne Lynch for their extensive knowledge of the city.

A special thanks to Graffiti King Andre Charles (A Charles) for his design of my cover. A Charles is one of the few "old school Kings" whose beautiful street scene murals send out positive messages across the cityscape in our neighborhoods. He is also one of the few who works strictly by permission and commission from the community. I hope to work with him again in the future.

The expertise of: My acting coach, LK Thompson, who helped me find my inner voice. My voice coach; Patrick Wickham of Wickham Vocal Studios, who helped me condition my voice for the long three hour tours. Lorraine Ferro; a singer and songwriter hall-of-famer, who helped tie a lot of the loose ends in this making together and Dr. Dick Breeze; Director of the English Theater Company (ETC), for his philosophy and worldly advice.

I have to especially thank our District Leader, the Honorable Jim R. McManus and the members of his democratic association who allowed me unfettered access to their library. Get the vote out guys! And thanks to the rest of my friends and family that bore with me through this arduous journey.

In short, everybody had a friend who had a friend, who knew somebody who helped me.

Thank you all.